Your
BEST
DAYS
are still
AHEAD

Your
BEST
DAYS
are still
AHEAD

DENNIS LEONARD

LEGACY
PUBLISHERS INTERNATIONAL

YOUR BEST DAYS ARE STILL AHEAD:
MOVING BEYOND YESTERDAY'S PAIN

Dennis Leonard
9495 East Florida Avenue
Denver, CO 80247
(303) 369-8514
www.DLministries.com

ISBN 1-880809-53-2
Printed in the United States of America
© 2006 by Dennis Leonard

Legacy Publishers International
1301 South Clinton Street
Denver, CO 80247
www.legacypublishersinternational.com

4 5 6 7 8 9 10 / 09 08 07 06

Dedication

This book is dedicated to all those who are sick and tired of being sick and tired—to those who can't see the light at the end of the tunnel because of the shadows of their past.

Know that God loves you and is not angry with you. Receive all that He has for you: health, prosperity, peace, and joy. It's time to rise up and walk into the future that God has planned for you.

> *"For I know the plans that I have for you," declares the LORD, "plans for welfare and not for calamity to give you a future and a hope."* (Jeremiah 29:11)

It's time to believe with me that your best days are still ahead.

Acknowledgments

I want to thank my beautiful wife, Michele, for her strength, courage, and unwavering love for me. Her unconditional support and encouragement continue to inspire me to be all that God has called me to be. With her by my side, I know that my best days are still ahead.

To my sons, Mark and Garret, who serve with me in the ministry, I am forever grateful to the Lord that you have chosen to use your God-given talents, so that together we can touch a hurting world with the love of Jesus Christ.

To the staff of Heritage Christian Center, thank you for your loyalty and support of the vision that God has given us; you have increased the measure of my life.

Most important, I want to acknowledge the Lord Jesus Christ in all my ways, for it is He who has directed my paths and constantly reassures me that both your best days and mine are still ahead.

Contents

Introduction

"Your Best Days Are Still Ahead"

We live in a negative world that tends to produce negative results in our lives. God wants you to know that through your faith in Him, you can live above the negativity that surrounds you.

Life is not always fair, but when you know what God says about your situation you can move beyond all the pain of your past. This book will show you how to let go of your issues and reach for the promises that God has for you today.

Maybe people close to you treated you unfairly. Maybe those who should have loved you did not. You do not have to live with that bitterness or unforgiveness in your life. Whatever negative issues are weighing you down today, this book will help you overcome them. God's Word tells us that we don't have to be enslaved by guilt, negativity, or even fear.

When you know the plans that God has for you then you will know that you don't have to live in the pain of your past. When you know that God has something great in store for you then you will know that your best days are still ahead.

Even if you have been caught in a cycle of failure or addictive behaviors, you can see everything turn around with God's help. Even if you've been greatly disappointed in life, you can find the life that you've always dreamed of.

This book is a life-changing message that you have been looking for. The principles outlined in these pages will help you get everything turned around in your life. The freedom you have always wanted is just around the corner.

I believe with all of my heart that when you learn and apply God's principles, "Your best days are still ahead."

Dennis Leonard

PART I

Breaking Free

At the very outset of this book, I want to present to you what I consider to be God's "divine scissors" that can cut the emotional strings that manipulate your life and make you a puppet of the enemy. These are foundational principles that relate to the rest of the book. Again and again, I am going to challenge you to use these five powerful tools that truly have the power to help you break free! These truths are:

- Faith

- Forgiveness

- A Renewed Mind

- God's Word

- Obedience

There are no substitutes for these concepts. They are the "means" that God has given us to defeat the enemy of our souls—not just once, but day in and day out.

There are no shortcuts to using these concepts in your life. And nobody can use them in your life *but* you. You must make a choice that you *will* walk by faith, you *will* forgive, you *will* choose to have a renewed mind and rely upon God's Word, and you *will* obey. The good news is this: What God commands you to do, He empowers you to do! You can break free of the ties that bind you, and then live free the rest of your life.

BREAKING FREE

1

The Power of Your Faith

S he was an unknown, unnamed, and unclean woman—an outcast in her society. She was identified primarily by her ailment—she had been hemorrhaging in miserable obscurity for twelve long and lonely years. But one day Jesus came to her town, and she managed to work her way through the crowds surrounding Him to touch the hem of His garment. He said to her, *"Daughter, take courage; your faith has made you well"* (Matt. 9:22).

And immediately, she was well.

Two blind men cried out to Jesus as He passed by, *"Have mercy on us, Son of David!"* (v. 27). When the men were brought to Jesus, He asked them, *"Do you believe that I am able to do this?"* (v. 28). They said to Him, *"Yes, Lord"* (v. 28). As He touched their eyes, He said, *"Be it done to you according to your faith"* (v. 29).

And immediately, their eyes were opened.

She was a "foreign woman," but she dared to cry out and to persist in crying out to Jesus for mercy on behalf of her demon-possessed daughter. Jesus said to her, *"Woman, your faith is great; be it done for you as you wish"* (Matt. 15:28).

And immediately, her daughter was healed.

Your Best Days Are Still Ahead

Time and again throughout His ministry, Jesus said to those who were in the grip of Satan, *"your faith"* will set you free of these ties that bind you.

Sometimes the ties were associated with physical ailments, sometimes with emotional or mental illness, sometimes with dark spiritual bondage. But, in each case, it was the activation and release of faith that made the difference.

If you truly desire to break free of the emotional bondage that is manipulating your life, you *must* choose to walk according to what God's Word says rather than according to how you feel, what the world says, or what the devil tempts you with. You *must* make a decision to walk by *faith*.

Faith Is Not a Feeling

Faith is an act of your *will*. It is a choice you make. It is a determination, a resolve, a commitment, a firm decision. Faith is saying, "I will choose to love God and follow God's commandments *regardless* of how I feel in any given moment."

There will be times when...

You will become discouraged in your work.

You will become discouraged in your giving.

You will become discouraged in your prayer.

You will become discouraged in your witness.

You will become discouraged in your believing.

There's an emotional "weariness" that can overtake a person to the degree that he no longer *wants* to make any effort to try again, try harder, or, in severe cases, even try to get up in the morning. Don't let that happen to you! It's in those very moments of weakness that you must activate your faith!

The flesh wants everything to be easy. The flesh operates according to "feelings" 99 percent of the time.

The flesh doesn't want to get up early to exercise. The flesh just doesn't "feel" like exercising.

The flesh doesn't want to show up an hour before church to pray. The flesh just doesn't "feel" like getting there early.

The flesh certainly doesn't want to tithe. The flesh doesn't want to "feel" *any* kind of sacrifice.

Walking by faith always involves a confrontation with the flesh. The flesh says "yes" to all kinds of lusts, passions, rebellions, and temptations. Faith says "no."

The flesh says "no" to discipline. Faith says "yes."

The flesh says "yes" to greed and pride and laziness. Faith says "no."

The flesh says "no" to going out of your way to help another person. Faith says "yes."

The flesh says "yes" to prejudice and bigotry. Faith says "no."

The flesh says "no" to kindness and mercy that are undeserved. Faith says "yes."

The flesh always compels us—with an obsessive, never-satisfied "drive"—to do what brings immediate gratification and pleasure. Faith always points us toward eternal rewards and toward those things that truly bring a sense of purpose and fulfillment.

The flesh always prompts us to think "physical need" and "material want" before we think "spiritual consequences." Faith always demands that we think "spiritual consequences" before we think "physical need" or "material want."

The flesh always wants to quit the minute the going gets tough. Faith says, "Keep going. Keep trusting God!"

Faith Is Not the World's Message

The world continually sends us the message, "Take the easiest route to the top. Use whatever shortcuts are available.

Manipulate whomever you need to manipulate. Con whomever you can con. Use a little deceit and tell a little lie if you need to. Do all that is in your power to be number one—number one among your friends, number one in your family, number one at work, number one in the church." The world's message is one of striving, of competition, of "using people and loving things" rather than "loving people and using things."

Faith takes the exact opposite approach. Faith says, "I will walk in a steadfast and godly manner even if the entire world is going the other direction." Faith says, "I will honor and respect and be compassionate toward other people. I will treat people in an honest way." Faith says, "I will be a giver and not a taker only."

Faith Is the Opposite of What the Devil Says

One of the devil's most frequently used lies is this: "Do what feels good." The devil will try to convince you that God "made" you with a dark side, an evil streak, a built-in desire for sin. He will continually tempt you to satisfy your fleshly nature—to "fulfill" all your inner longings, passions, desires, and wants—no matter who you may hurt or how you may be fueling your own demise in the end.

The devil will never tell you the whole truth about any sin—he can't tell the truth; it's not his nature. He will never tell you that the first drink you take can lead you down a road to alcoholism. He will never tell you that the first hit can lead to an addiction. He will never tell you that you can get pregnant the first time you have sex. He will never tell you that you are heading for major heartache and sometimes serious illness when you engage in something you know is "wrong."

No, the devil's lie is, "Live in the moment, and do what feels good to you *now*."

Faith says, "I will live with an eye toward eternity. I will live in a way that will eventually bring me God's highest and best blessings. I will say 'no' to anything that is contrary to God's commandments, and I will say 'yes' to everything that is in keeping with His promises."

Faith Is "Living Out" What God Says

God's Word tells us *"we walk by faith, not by sight"* (2 Cor. 5:7).

What does it mean to walk by faith? First, let me tell you what it *doesn't* mean. It doesn't mean that we live in denial of reality. It doesn't mean that we toss our bills into the trash can and hope they will go away. It doesn't mean that we turn a blind eye to the sinfulness around us and hope that things will get better. It doesn't mean that we ignore warning signs that God allows us to see. Rather, it means that even in dire situations, we believe God will cause everything to turn out all right.

The Christian walk is real. It is practical and daily and meant to be lived out in a real world among real people encountering real situations.

Let me remind you of what the apostle Paul wrote to the Corinthians just before he said, *"we walk by faith, not by sight."* He wrote that we *"groan"* and are *"burdened"* (v. 2, 4) because we live in fleshly bodies and in a fallen world. He wrote about how we long to live in heaven with God and to escape all that is temporal and troublesome. He told how we have a built-in desire to be with the Lord and not to have to deal with the problems all around us. The apostle Paul never turned a blind eye to the troubles of this life.

But then he said, *"He who prepared us for this very purpose"*—which is living in this troublesome earth with heaven as our future home—*"is God, who gave to us the Spirit as a pledge"* (v. 5).

God has given us the Holy Spirit so we might face our problems and overcome them. He has given us the Holy Spirit so we might have courage as we engage in the battles of each day's temptations, trials, and troubles. Paul wrote, *"Therefore, being always of good courage,...we have as our ambition...to be pleasing to Him"* (2 Cor. 5:6, 9). God's Word also says, *"Without faith it is impossible to please Him* [God]*"* (Heb. 11:6).

We don't deny our problems. They exist. But we have heaven as our *goal* and our future home. And we have "pleasing God" as our *purpose* and our *reason* for trusting Him day to day.

Faith Is a Decision

If faith is not a feeling, what is faith? It is always a decision made with the *will*.

Nothing connected to your faith is a feeling.

To walk by faith is a decision.

To forgive is a decision.

To attend church, to read your Bible, to pray, to speak what God says rather than what you feel, to give your tithe, to get involved in any ministry outreach is a *decision* you make. It is an act of your will.

It doesn't matter how you *feel* in any given situation. It matters what you decide to *do* in the midst of that situation.

Jesus said plainly, *"Have faith in God"* (Mark 11:22). In saying that, Jesus was clearly saying, "You have a choice—to have faith or not have faith. It is something you *decide*." Faith is a matter of saying, "God said it. I believe it. I speak it out of my mouth. I act on it! I live by faith."

Because faith is a decision that *you* make, and nobody else makes for you, it is one thing that nobody and no circumstance can take from you. Faith doesn't rise and fall according to circumstances. It can remain steady and focused and strong even in the worst of situations.

Faith Is a "Walk"

Nobody ever experiences all the faith he will ever need for the rest of his life in one flash of power. Our faith rises up and is used as we live out our lives minute by minute, hour by hour, day by day. Faith is a "walk." It is taking life one step at a time, believing God that as we take a step, He will give us the energy to take the *next* step.

Through the years, I have met a number of people who were once addicted to a chemical substance. One thought that every recovering addict lives with the rest of his life is this: "Live one day at a time."

That's exactly what Jesus taught. He said, *"Do not be anxious for tomorrow; for tomorrow will care for itself. Each day has enough trouble of its own"* (Matt. 6:34).

Faith operates as we make one decision at a time.

Faith functions as we make one choice at a time.

Faith functions as we solve one problem at a time.

Faith functions from conversation to conversation…chore to chore…appointment to appointment…hour by hour.

In each decision, each choice, each problem, each encounter or bit of work, we ask, "What would God like for me to do?"

We've all seen the letters WWJD in recent years—"What Would Jesus Do." Those letters WWJD are on everything from bumper stickers to bracelets to fancy office plaques. The question "What would Jesus do?" can become almost a cliché unless we are careful. The question is one we each need to ask with great sincerity and with eyes, ears, and heart open to receive God's answer.

When you are facing several options, ask, "What choice would Jesus make?"

When you are in a dilemma, ask, "Which path would Jesus follow?"

When you are confronted with temptations, ask, "Which choice would Jesus make?"

As you go to an appointment, meet with a friend or business colleague, run an errand, or face a mountain of paperwork, ask, "What would Jesus like for me to say or do?"

And then, the moment you discern what it is that Jesus wants you to do, the second statement of faith is, "I'm trusting You, Lord, to *help* me do what You have shown me to do."

Walking by faith means asking the Lord to lead and guide you—not just once in a lifetime or once a week, but moment by moment.

Walking by faith means trusting God to help you to live in such a way that you bring glory to His name and blessing to your own life.

Walking by faith means recognizing that God is with you always, that He *desires* to show you the right paths to follow, and that He *desires* to help you accomplish anything He sets before you to do.

Faith says to your heart and mind, "I believe God loves me and will care for me *all the way through every ordeal and every triumph* of this life. He will be with me every moment of every day until I am in heaven with Him. God is ultimately in charge of every aspect of my life, and He will walk with me and give me courage to face anything I have to face."

A Walk of Strength and Power

Every person I know who truly walks by faith has a tremendous inner strength. Faith is potent!

"But," you may be saying, "I don't think I have much faith."

You have *enough* faith for where you are today and what you are experiencing right now. God gives to every person *"a measure of faith"* (Rom. 12:3).

22

Most people I know are closer to their victory than they think.

They are stronger than they think.

They have more faith than they think they have.

Believe that God has put into you the precise measure of faith you need to believe for the maximum amount of reward He has prepared for you.

Believe that God has the enduring strength you need to persist in your prayers and in your giving and in your witness until you receive that reward.

Believe that God has the victory you desire in your future and that you are one day closer to that victory today than you were yesterday.

Persist in your faith. God calls us to persevere, to have enduring power.

So many people give up too soon! They use their faith and when they don't see immediate results, they throw up their hands and conclude, "Faith doesn't work." In truth, it *does* work if you will only persist in your believing.

Everybody around you may fail you.

Your spouse may fail you.

Your employer may fail you.

Your neighbor may fail you.

Your friend may fail you.

Your pastor may fail you.

But God will never fail you. And He has given you faith that will not fail if you use it and endure in using it.

Use Your Faith until the Desired Change Comes

Jesus said that our faith has tremendous power to change external circumstances around us. He taught:

> *Truly I say to you, whoever says to this mountain, "Be taken up and cast into the sea," and does not doubt in his heart, but believes that what he says is going to happen, it shall be granted him. Therefore I say to you, all things for which you pray and ask, believe that you have received them, and they shall be granted you.* (Mark 11:23–24)

The word *"believe"* in this passage could be translated "believe and keep on believing." Walking in faith requires perseverance. It requires a commitment never to "give up" in weariness or "give in" to temptations. God's Word says, *"Let us not lose heart in doing good, for in due time we shall reap if we do not grow weary"* (Gal. 6:9).

Get your eyes off today's situation. If you dwell on today's misery, you are going to start magnifying that misery in your mind and heart and, eventually, it will blot out all ideas and all goals that are related to a bright future. If you allow thoughts associated with your present misery to loom so large that they wipe out your dreams and your understanding about what God desires for you, you will become paralyzed and weak. You will develop an inner weariness in your soul that will keep you from making any effort whatsoever.

Faith does work, but a key aspect of faith is *faithfulness*. You need to keep using your faith, and keep using it, and keep using it. Jesus said, *"Ask, and it shall be given to you; seek, and you shall find; knock, and it shall be opened to you. For everyone who asks receives, and he who seeks finds, and to him who knocks it shall be opened"* (Matt. 7:7).

The Greek language in which the New Testament was originally written is actually much clearer in this passage than what we have in many of our English translations. The tense of the verbs in the Greek language is such that this verse is perhaps better stated this way:

> Ask, and keep on asking and keep on asking, and it shall be given to you. Seek, and keep on seeking and keep

on seeking, and you shall find. Knock, and keep on knocking and keep on knocking, and it shall be opened to you. For every one who asks and keeps on asking receives, and he who seeks and keeps on seeking finds, and to him who knocks and keeps on knocking it shall be opened.

Jesus taught perseverance and endurance. He said very plainly, *"It is the one who has endured to the end who will be saved"* (Matt. 10:22). Jesus wasn't speaking only about the eternal salvation of our souls in that verse. He was referring to those who stand and continue to stand with faith in the face of all sorts of persecution and hatred.

If you don't quit asking, God *will* answer.

If you don't quit seeking, God *will* show you the way.

If you don't quit knocking, God *will* open the door to you.

That answer—that way, that open door—will always be one that is for your good.

Seek to Grow in Your Faith

One of the most faithful and spiritually strong women I have ever met or heard about was a woman known as "Aunt Bessie." She was a pillar of her church—eighty-nine years old and still going strong. She had a special ministry of playing the piano for the "old people" at the church-sponsored retirement center. This meant, of course, that Aunt Bessie went three times a week to play hymns and gospel songs for "old people" who were twenty years younger than she was!

If any need came up in the church, Aunt Bessie was the first to say, "Well, let's just take that to Jesus."

If she was given bad news, Aunt Bessie's first response was, "Well, I'm going to have to talk to Jesus about that."

If she struggled in any area of her life—her health, her income, her family—and somebody asked her about her

25

troubles, Aunt Bessie could be counted on to reply, "Jesus is taking care of that."

One day a pastor asked Aunt Bessie about her faith. He asked her if she had ever wavered in her faith. She said, "Oh, yes. When I was a young woman, I often would go to God and say, 'I know You can do this, but what I'm wondering is if You will.'"

"Is that still the way you talk to God?" the pastor asked.

"Oh, no!" Aunt Bessie said with a steely glint in her eye. "When I was about thirty, I said that to God and He spoke right back to me, 'Bessie, I don't deal in *if*s and *but*s. I deal in what, when, where, and how.'"

Aunt Bessie went on, "So I started changing my prayers. I said, 'God, I know You can do this. I'm going to trust You to do what's best, and to do it when You want to do it and how You want to do it. Just show me where I need to be to receive it.' And that's the way I've lived the last fifty-eight years."

This pastor continued, "Then Aunt Bessie looked me right in the eye and said, 'Young man, God still deals in what, when, where, and how. Don't ever forget it. Your job isn't to figure out life—your job is to know God and let *Him* figure out your life.'"

What wisdom!

The truth of God's Word from cover to cover is that your level of faith is always directly related to your relationship with Jesus Christ.

It's related to the times you spend in prayer to Him.

It's related to the degree you are willing to trust Him.

It's related to the degree you believe that what He has said, He will do.

It's related to how much you are going to rely on Him to determine the what, when, where, and how—and to help you be where you need to be to receive all He has for you!

If you have a problem in your life, begin to see it in this light: Your problem today has been allowed by God so that you may grow in your faith.

You may think your problem is all about your spouse and what he or she is doing or not doing. You may think your problem today is all about your bills that aren't being paid. Your problem is actually a faith exercise. God is building you up to trust Him with the what, when, and how of your life. He is molding you so you will be where He wants you to be at precisely the right moment He wants you to be there.

The emotions that the devil uses to manipulate you are discouragement, fear, doubt, and anxiety; they keep you from using your faith. True freedom comes when we *believe* God and *keep believing* Him.

The person who walks by faith is no longer ruled by his emotions. He is able to move beyond yesterday's pain.

A Prayer to Activate Your Faith

I encourage you to make this your prayer today:

Heavenly Father, eternal God, thank You for sending Your only begotten Son, Jesus Christ, to die for me on the cross. I believe in Jesus and accept His forgiveness and His gift of eternal life. From this moment forward, I make the decision to walk by faith in Him, and not give in to the fear I feel.

Father, I trust that Your power is greater than any force of the devil against my life. I ask You to take complete authority over the spirit of depression that has me in its grip. I ask You to break every hold the devil has on my life. I open my life right now to receive Your help and Your joy.

Father, I praise You for your faithfulness to me. I praise You for delivering me. Help me now to walk in faith according to Your Word. In the name of Jesus, I will no longer live by my feelings. I will embrace new hope for my future. I will not allow tension, anxiety, depression, or worry to overtake me. I will trust You to help me do all the things You call me to do.

Thank You for giving me a spirit of joy and enthusiasm for the life You desire for me to live in the minutes, hours, days, weeks, months, and years that lie ahead. I proclaim by the power of the Holy Spirit within me that *my best days are still ahead.* I will walk toward my destiny with great energy, enthusiasm, and passion. I declare today that the *joy* of the Lord is my strength.

I pray all this in Jesus' name. Amen!

Also, let me encourage you to log on to my website, www.dennisleonardministries.com, and click on the "Prayer Chapel" icon. Send me your prayer requests so that we can pray and agree together over the needs in your life.

2

The Power of Forgiveness

Our world is filled with injustices. At times, the injustices can seem to be such a violation of our most basic rights that we think, "That's beyond anyone's ability to forgive." God says that nothing is beyond our ability to forgive.

I saw a news program some time ago about a young boy who had thrown a rock through a man's window. The man chased after this boy with a gun, and he shot and killed the boy.

Now the normal reaction of most people in this world would be to seek revenge and to hold hatred and unforgiveness. This boy's parents took a very different approach. They began to pray for the man who had killed their son, and they decided to forgive him.

Many people who heard about what these parents did just shook their heads and said, "I couldn't do that." Some were bold enough to ask the parents, "How *could* you do that?"

The parents replied, "We had to. God said so."

The Command to Have a Forgiving Heart

The Christian doesn't have an option when it comes to forgiveness. God demands forgiveness from us. If a person is truly going to break free from the emotional pain that influences his or her life, he must forgive. We must forgive those who are in our past, as well as those who are in our present. Any person who has ever hurt you in any way is a person you need to forgive. Any person against whom you are holding any kind of grudge, resentment, or anger is a person you *must* forgive.

Jesus commanded His followers, *"Be merciful, just as your Father is merciful. And do not judge and you will not be judged; and do not condemn, and you will not be condemned; pardon, and you will be pardoned"* (Luke 6:36–37).

Jesus also taught, *"If you forgive men for their transgressions, your heavenly Father will also forgive you. But if you do not forgive men, then your Father will not forgive your transgressions"* (Matt. 6:14–15).

God's Word makes it very clear that our forgiveness of others who have hurt us is absolutely necessary if we are to know the joy of the Lord. Holding on to unforgiveness grieves the Holy Spirit.

Many people today are experiencing depression because they are holding on to negative emotions that God desires for them to release to Him. They are refusing to forgive, and in refusing to forgive, they are denying God the opportunity to heal the wounds they have deep inside their hearts.

As you learn how to walk in close fellowship with the Lord, one of the lessons He is going to teach you again and again is this: You have to let some things go!

You have to let go of the negative emotions you are feeling toward those who may have hurt you or disappointed you.

You have to let go of the insults and criticisms that have been leveled at you by those who sought your downfall.

You have to let go of the words of rejection that were intended to alienate or deter you.

You have to let go of everything negative that has been said about you or to you, as well as everything negative that has been done to you. Letting go of the sins that have been committed against you is absolutely essential for you to be made whole inside—for you to be filled with strength and confidence and boldness and authority and joy and every other manifestation of power and emotional healing that the Lord has for you.

God calls us repeatedly to forgive others. Just as you have been forgiven by the Lord Jesus, so you must forgive. An unbeliever doesn't have the real ability to forgive others. The Lord expects those who have received His forgiveness, however, to forgive others.

There's no type of sin too horrific for God to forgive.

There's no amount of sin too great for God to forgive.

There's no length of time spent in sin that is too long for God to forgive.

It is God's nature to forgive *in spite of* what a person has done. That must become our nature, too.

God's forgiveness covers *all* sin in those who come to Him and confess their sin and seek His mercy. God's Word declares, *"If we confess our sins, He is faithful and righteous to forgive us our sins and to cleanse us from all unrighteousness"* (1 John 1:9).

In like manner, then, we are never justified in saying that any sin is too horrific, too great, or too long-standing for us to forgive. We must forgive because we have been forgiven.

What Does Forgiveness Really Mean?

Many people are confused about what forgiveness means, so let's be very clear on that point. Forgiveness means "release."

It doesn't mean that you weren't hurt—to forgive does not mean that you are denying that you felt pain or were injured in some way.

Forgiveness doesn't mean that the actions of another person were inconsequential or insignificant. Forgiveness also doesn't mean that you refuse to hold a person accountable in a court of law if the law of the land has been broken.

Forgiveness means to open up your heart and mind and *release* the person who has hurt you. More specifically, it calls for you to release that person into the hands of almighty God.

God knows fully what to do for that person, to that person, and about that person! Trust Him to act on your behalf. Don't take vengeance into your own hands. The Lord tells us in His Word: *"Vengeance is Mine, and retribution"* (Deut. 32:35).

When you don't forgive another person, you are putting yourself in the position of judge, jury, and warden of the prison. You are taking on responsibility that belongs to God alone!

Trust God to be the judge of that person. Trust God to be the jury that hears his or her case and determines just consequences. Trust God to enforce *His* consequences.

Even in "Undeserving Cases"

"But the person doesn't deserve to be forgiven," you may say.

Let me remind you that you didn't *deserve* to be forgiven of any of your sins either. No person can *earn* or *deserve* God's forgiveness. God's Word says, *"God demonstrates His own love toward us, in that while we were yet sinners, Christ died for us"* (Rom. 5:8). God was motivated by love and mercy to send His Son, Jesus Christ, to die on a cross so that when we believe in Jesus and accept His death as being on our behalf, He forgives us completely. Jesus spoke of God's motivation when He said, *"God so loved the world, that He gave His only begotten Son, that whoever believes in Him should not perish, but have eternal life"* (John 3:16).

I assure you that your mind will always work against you when it comes to forgiveness. Your mind will fight you, saying, "It's not fair. That person doesn't deserve to be forgiven. That person hurt me. I hope he gets what he deserves."

It's the replaying of those ideas over and over again that keeps you from "forgetting."

Let it go!

Say to the Lord, "It doesn't seem fair. But I'm trusting You to do what is just."

Say to the Lord, "It's really hard for me to forgive. But I'm trusting You to be my Defender and my Advocate."

Say to the Lord, "I'm hurting. Please, heal me."

One of the reasons we don't let go of a person is because we don't think God knows, or God cares, about what has happened to us. Let me remind you of what the Lord said in His Word to His people:

> *You shall not wrong a stranger or oppress him, for you were strangers in the land of Egypt. You shall not afflict any widow or orphan. If you afflict him at all, and if he does cry out to Me, I will surely hear his cry; and My anger will be kindled, and I will kill you with the sword; and your wives shall become widows and your children fatherless. If you lend money to My people, to the poor among you, you are not to act as a creditor to him; you shall not charge him interest. If you ever take your neighbor's cloak as a pledge, you are to return it to him before the sun sets, for that is his only covering; it is his cloak for his body. What else shall he sleep in? And it shall come about that when he cries out to Me, I will hear him, for I am gracious.* (Exod. 22:21–27)

This passage tells us that God *sees* what you do to your neighbors—He sees how you mistreat people, how you put heavy burdens on them, how you take from them. He says, "If your neighbor cries out to Me, I will listen with a compassionate ear." He says, "I will execute justice on you for the way you mistreat other people."

Turn that around. If God hears your neighbor cry out against you, surely He hears you cry out against your neighbor!

The person who has mistreated you, placed a heavy burden on you, stolen from you, or in any way hurt you has far more to fear from the hand of God than anything you could ever do to that person!

No, our motivation in forgiving is never because the other person "deserves" forgiveness. Rather, our motivation for forgiving is our love for God. The Bible tells us,

> *Beloved, if God so loved us, we also ought to love one another....We love, because He first loved us. If someone says, "I love God," and hates his brother, he is a liar....This commandment we have from Him that the one who loves God should love his brother also.* (1 John 4:11, 19–21)

Forgiving Is for Our Benefit

Many people seem to think that forgiveness is doing somebody else a "favor." To the contrary. It is doing yourself a favor!

Forgiving is not for the benefit of the one whom we forgive. It is for our benefit. Forgiveness frees us in our souls. It liberates us from the bondage of old hurtful memories. It restores what has been damaged in us. It brings about healing and comfort and a renewal of feelings of value and worthiness.

Forgetting, Too

Even as Christians, we sometimes find ourselves saying, "Well, I forgive—but I can't forget."

If you don't *forget*, you will continue to hold that person hostage in your mind and heart. The fact is, you are still hoping that something bad will happen to that person to punish him or her for hurting you.

The unfortunate truth about holding another person hostage in your mind and heart is that *you* are the one who is actually the hostage. When you can't let go of ideas and images from the past that haunt you, when you can't release pain from your heart, when you can't forget the sound of stinging words that cut you to the core, *you* become the victim. You are the one who remains in torment over what has been done to you.

The lingering thoughts of past injustices, abuse, rejection, ridicule, criticism, or any other type of "trespass" against your life will tie you up, hold you back, and keep you down. Any time you do not release others who have hurt you, you build a wall of pain around your life, and *you* are the prisoner kept within those self-built walls.

Unforgiveness breeds terrible emotions in the human heart—

- Bitterness

- Hatred

- Rage

These three emotions are like poison to your spirit and soul. They create a toxic environment that makes praise and joy nearly impossible. They seep into your language and behavior and generate still further guilt, shame, and sorrow in your heart and life. The cycle is one that spirals downward.

The longer you hold on to unforgiveness, the more bitterness, hatred, and rage you will feel. The more you feel these emotions, the more you will feel, speak, and act in an ungodly manner. And the more you speak and act in ways that are contrary to God's purposes for your life, the more you are going to justify your unforgiveness and breed still more bitterness, hatred, and rage. The end result is that you end up with far greater injury than the person who hurt you will *ever* experience, even if that person is convicted, imprisoned, or executed!

In addition, there are two very negative trends that become established in your life when you refuse to forgive.

First, when you refuse to forgive another person, you set yourself up to be hurt by just that type of person in the future. I see this happen time and time again. A person may be divorced by a spouse, or may be the one doing the divorcing, and then turn right around and marry another person who is amazingly like the person he or she was married to previously!

If you have been the victim of a person in the past, you are much more likely to become the victim of just that type of person in the future.

If you have been abused by a person in the past, you are much more likely to be abused by just that type of person in the future.

Forgiveness breaks this cycle! It frees you so you can stand confidently and boldly and say "No" to those who abuse you. It frees you so you can say, "I will not be your victim." It frees you so you can say, "You hurt me. I will not stand by and let you continue to hurt me."

Second, when you refuse to forgive another person, you are much more likely to become the very same type of person as the person who has hurt you. I also see this happen again and again. Children who are abused by their parents and refuse to forgive those parents tend to become parents who abuse their own children. Employees who feel hurt from the disrespect of an employer or a supervisor tend to become supervisors who disrespect and hurt those who are put under their supervision.

Forgiveness is the number-one way to break this cycle as well. Forgiveness gives you the freedom to choose a different way of responding. It allows you to let go of past harmful patterns in your life so you can learn, embrace, and live out new loving and helpful patterns of thinking, believing, feeling, speaking, and behaving.

Jesus told a parable about forgiveness:

The kingdom of heaven may be compared to a certain king who wished to settle accounts with his slaves. And when he had begun to settle them, there was brought to him one who owed him ten thousand talents. But since he did not have the means to repay, his lord commanded him to be sold, along with his wife and children and all that he had, and repayment to be made. The slave therefore falling down, prostrated himself before him, saying, "Have patience with me, and I will repay you everything." And the lord of that slave felt compassion and released him and forgave him the debt. But that slave went out and found one of his fellow slaves who owed him a hundred denarii; and he seized him and began to choke him, saying, "Pay back what you owe." So his fellow slave fell down and began to entreat him, saying, "Have patience with me and I will repay you." He was unwilling however, but went and threw him in prison until he should pay back what was owed. So when his fellows slaves saw what had happened, they were deeply grieved and came and reported to their lord all that had happened. Then summoning him, his lord said to him, "You wicked slave, I forgave you all that debt because you entreated me. Should you not also have had mercy on your fellow slave, even as I had mercy on you?" And his lord, moved with anger, handed him over to the torturers until he should repay all that was owed him. (Matt. 18:23–34)

Jesus concluded this parable by saying, *"So shall My heavenly Father also do to you, if each of you does not forgive his brother from your heart"* (v. 35).

Unforgiveness will plunge your life into an emotional "prison." It will keep you from experiencing the freedom Christ has provided for you. Unforgiveness results in a dark dungeon of the soul. It produces emotional anguish or "torture."

When we refuse to forgive, we do *not* have the upper hand in the situation. The exact opposite is true—we lose even more, we hurt and suffer even deeper, we feel even greater despair.

Jesus said about those who crucified Him, "Father, forgive them. They don't know what they are doing." (See Luke 23:34.) Those are the very words we must pray. "Father, forgive that person! He didn't know what he was doing."

And, in truth, the person who hurt you didn't really know what he was doing. Oh, he may have been conscious and mentally sane. He may even have been willful in what he did, but he really didn't know the full consequences of what He was doing in God's eyes. He didn't know where his sin would take him, not only in this life but from eternity's perspective. He really didn't know how much damage he was doing to himself in hurting you.

Make a decision to forgive those who have hurt you in any way. Chalk their error up to the fact that they didn't know what they were doing—not really, not eternally, not spiritually.

Forgiveness Brings Freedom and Joy

Consider the life of Joseph, the eleventh son of Jacob. Joseph was terribly wronged. His brothers in their jealousy sold him into slavery. His employer, in a rage that came about as a result of a lie, had him thrown into prison. A fellow prisoner, who could have helped him if he had remembered to help him, *kept* him in prison. If anybody ever had a good reason to harbor unforgiveness in his heart, it was Joseph.

Joseph easily could have said, "I didn't deserve this. I've been wronged. I've been denied the justice I deserve." He could have allowed thoughts such as these to tie him in knots, with the result being great bitterness, anger, and hatred.

We have no evidence, however, that Joseph ever thought any of those negative thoughts or felt any of those negative emotions. In fact, there's evidence to suggest just the opposite because people who are filled with bitterness, anger, and hatred are rarely, if ever, promoted by others in authority over them to positions of leadership. And whether it was in Potiphar's house or in an Egyptian prison, Joseph rose to the top. He was put in leadership positions where he repeatedly worked for the blessing and welfare of others.

All along the way, Joseph trusted God. He saw God as being totally in control of His life. He saw God as the One who helped him interpret the dreams of his fellow prisoners, and eventually Pharaoh's dreams. Joseph refused to live with unforgiveness.

After almost twelve years of fighting the rats, heat, and sickness of a Middle East prison, Joseph was miraculously freed and put in the position of being the number-two leader in Egypt. When a famine hit the region, Joseph's brothers came to him requesting food. He held no ill will against them. Rather, he said to them,

> *Do not be grieved or angry with yourselves, because you sold me here; for God sent me before you to preserve life...to preserve for you a remnant in the earth, and to keep you alive by a great deliverance. Now, therefore, it was not you who sent me here, but God.* (Gen. 45:5, 7–8)

Joseph "freed" his brothers from any guilt and regret they had. He freely forgave them. And, in so doing, he freed himself from the loneliness of being separated from his father and other family members.

Not only that, but as Joseph released his brothers with his words of forgiveness, he also released the tremendous power of love. God's Word says,

Then he [Joseph] fell on his brother Benjamin's neck and wept; and Benjamin wept on his neck. And he kissed all his brothers and wept on them, and afterward his brothers talked with him. (Gen. 45:14–15)

Don't miss this very important point:

Forgiveness releases the power of God. When the power of God is flowing freely in your life—when you have escaped from your self-imposed prison and are no longer enslaved by hatred and unforgiveness...

Bitterness is replaced by joy.

Hatred is replaced by love.

Anger is replaced by deep peace.

Revenge is replaced with acts of compassionate giving.

And in an atmosphere marked by joy, love, peace, and compassionate giving, lives are transformed!

Husbands and wives experience renewal and restoration in their marriages.

Mothers-in-law and daughters-in-law get along.

Parents and children stop fighting and experience harmony at home.

Employers and employees are able to work together instead of against each other.

People of all cultures and backgrounds start to worship together and work hand in hand for the benefit of their church and community.

People who haven't spoken to each other for years initiate conversations with one another.

The walls that have been built up and have become obstacles to the miracle-working power of God are broken down by forgiveness. When people are freely forgiving one another and moving into relationships marked by love, joy, peace, compassion, and giving, the result is a great and sweeping flow of God's saving, delivering, healing, restoring, and renewing power!

Yes, in an atmosphere marked by joy, love, peace, and compassionate giving, marriages and families are strengthened, companies are improved, churches are revitalized, and communities are transformed! Forgiveness sets in motion a tremendous release of God's power.

The Practical Steps *after* Forgiveness

Forgiveness doesn't begin and end in a person's heart or attitude. It doesn't begin and end with a person saying, "I forgive you." God requires more than that for us to be *fully* free of the ties that the devil would seek to use in binding and manipulating us.

What is God's full answer for unforgiveness?

Recognize that when you hold unforgiveness against a person, you are making that person an "enemy." You think of him as an enemy, you feel about him the way you feel about an enemy, you treat him as an enemy, you avoid him in the way you try to avoid an enemy, and you want his defeat because you count him an enemy.

Jesus made it very clear how we are to treat our enemies. He gave three great commandments regarding the response we are to make:

1. Love your enemy.

Jesus said, *"Love your enemies"* (Luke 6:27).

Change the image that you have had of that person. See him or her as a sinner, just as you once were, in need of mercy and forgiveness. See that person as a "work in progress," just as you are, and as someone with deep spiritual and emotional needs, just as you have needs.

So often we see those who have hurt us as being strong, powerful, invincible, as unrelenting tyrants. See them the way God sees them: weak, finite, miserable in their sin, damaged in their emotions, and in need of great forgiveness and healing.

2. Do good to your enemy.

Jesus said plainly, *"Do good to those who hate you"* (Luke 6:27). Furthermore, Jesus made doing good a very practical matter. He taught:

• If a person curses you, speak well of him in return.

• If a person hits you on one cheek, offer him your other cheek as well.

• If he takes your jacket, offer him your top coat, too.

• If he asks you to carry a burden one mile, carry it for two miles.

• If he demands something from you, give it freely. (See Luke 6:28–35 and Matthew 5:39–44.)

Jesus said that no matter what an enemy does to you, treat that person with *mercy*. (See Luke 6:36.)

3. Pray for your enemy.

Jesus said, *"Pray for those who persecute you in order that you may be sons of your Father who is in heaven"* (Matt. 5:44–45).

Pray that God will bring every evil intention, motive, or idea to light so that it might be recognized as evil.

Pray that God will get hold of your enemy's heart and convict him of his sin. Pray for the salvation of your enemy. Stop to think about it—if your enemy truly turns to God, he no longer will turn *on* you in hatred, but rather, will eventually turn *toward* you with love and kindness.

Pray that God will change his attitude.

Pray that God will change the way this person speaks to you and acts toward you. Pray, too, that God will change his attitude so that he will no longer criticize you or ridicule you in his conversations with others.

Pray that God will meet your enemy's deep emotional needs. The fact is, when the emotional needs in this person's life are met, he will act in a far different way toward you!

Pray that God will stay your enemy's hand so he cannot act toward you with violence or bring harm to any of your loved ones or your property.

Pray that God will surround your enemy with people who will influence him for *good*.

A man named Roderick once told me that he *thought* he had forgiven his father until he heard me tell the full story of forgiveness. He said, "Bishop, I just don't think I can do the rest of this."

I knew from previous conversations with Roderick that he had been terribly abused both physically and emotionally by his father. His father had routinely beaten him, often when he was in a drunken rage, and he had rarely said a kind word to him. He continually told Roderick what he couldn't do, wouldn't be able to do, and shouldn't even try to do. It was amazing to me that Roderick had succeeded in his life to the degree that he had. I credited Roderick's loving and supportive wife for much of his emotional healing.

Roderick told me that he had "released" his father some years before. But I knew from watching him and hearing how he interacted with others that Roderick wasn't fully free of his father's influence. I said to him that day, "Are you willing to *try* what I've said?"

"What do you mean?" Roderick said.

"Are you willing to try to love your father, do good to him, and pray for him?"

43

He said he was willing to *try,* so I referred him to a man who specializes in counseling people who have been abused as children. I could hardly believe the change in Roderick when I talked with him six months later. He was a man who now walked with far greater boldness and confidence. He was quick to smile and reach out to other people. As he shook my hand with a firm, eager grip, I asked, "What's happened to you?"

Roderick said, "Bishop, I did what you said and what the counselor said. The counselor asked me to see my father as a little baby and to pick him up and hold him like I hold my own boys. I don't mind telling you, that was hard. But when I did that, I felt such love for my dad I couldn't believe it. I saw that the only time my father had been truly 'himself' was when he was a baby—which was before his father and mother had abused *him.* I cried a lot that day, Bishop.

"Then I went to see my dad. He's in a nursing home. He's not only sick physically but he's lost a lot of his mental ability. I walked in and saw him sitting in a wheelchair, and I felt the same compassion I had felt when I imagined holding him as a baby. I didn't treat him as the father who had hit me and spoken negatively to me all my life. I treated him as that wounded little baby. The most amazing thing happened—my dad actually smiled at me. I think it was the first time I'd ever seen him smile at me.

"I asked him that day if I could pray for him, and he said I could. I prayed that God would heal him and protect him and take care of him. I prayed for him just like I pray for my own little boys. When I finished, my dad took my hand and grasped it hard. He had tears in his eyes. He didn't say anything, but he didn't have to.

"Bishop, I walked out of that nursing home a changed man."

He didn't even have to tell me that—I could see it!

The Full Freedom of Full Forgiveness

When you truly and fully forgive a person by beginning to love that person, do good to that person, and pray for that person, there's full freedom.

You no longer have to hold on to the memory of the hurt you felt. You no longer have to hold on to the pain. You no longer have to feel bound by what once happened to you.

When you give full forgiveness, you receive not only God's forgiveness from your own sin of trying to be "God" in another person's life, but you also receive the full freedom that God desires for you. You receive...

Freedom to move forward in your life.

Freedom to reach out to others with love, not hate.

Freedom to walk boldly and confidently in all situations, rather than be looking over your shoulder in fear that the person who hurt you may be in the room.

Freedom to speak about anybody, without feeling tension, anxiety, or vengeance in your soul.

There's an incredible sense of both freedom and power that will come to your heart when you fully pardon another person for the pain he or she has caused you. There's amazing freedom and power that will come to you when you are able to look into the face of a person who has hurt you and say, "I forgive you." There's awesome freedom and power that will come to you when you can confront the person who has taken something from you that you cherished and say, "I release you. I forgive you."

If a person has stolen your hopes and dreams, forgiving that person will open the door of your heart to new hopes and dreams.

If a person has rejected you and wounded your heart, forgiving that person will open the door of your heart to new love.

Your Best Days Are Still Ahead

Examine Your Heart Today

Examine your own life for signals that there's somebody you need to forgive.

Are you giving someone the "silent treatment?" That's a person you need to forgive.

Do you feel great tension inside, perhaps even seething anger, when you hear a person's name or see a person from a distance? That's a person you need to forgive.

Do you feel "cold" inside at the memory of a particular person? That's a person you need to forgive.

Do you desire to take out revenge on a person for what he or she has done to you or a loved one? That's a person you need to forgive.

Do you long to see a person suffer or experience a disaster of any type? That's a person you need to forgive.

All these are signals that you are holding something deep inside you that needs to be released, healed, or restored. The key to your experiencing the freedom, healing, and restoration you desire is forgiveness.

Refuse to be manipulated by the emotions linked to unforgiveness. Break free, because your best days are still ahead!

A Prayer to Activate Forgiveness

I encourage you to pray today:

Father, thank You for sending Jesus so that I might be saved eternally and freed in my spirit to love and serve You.

I believe You care for me and You desire for me to be healed of any past hurts in my life.

Free me from the bondage of unforgiveness. Remove this spirit of unforgiveness from my heart.

46

Help me to walk in love and boldness. Help me to treat those who have hurt me with kindness. Help me to do good to them and pray for them.

Heal me, Lord, and make me whole.

3

The Power of a Renewed Mind

The story is told of a little boy who was caught stealing apples from a neighbor's apple tree. His mother asked him why he had taken the apples and he said, "I took a different way home from school today."

His mother said, "What does that have to do with climbing Mr. Davis' tree and taking some of his apples?"

The boy said, "I walked home down Second Street by the bakery. Something smelled real good so I went inside. The lady said they had just finished baking apple pies."

The mother asked, "Were you hoping that I'd bake you one?"

"No," the little boy said. "I was hoping those apples would taste like pie!"

Disobedience always starts in your mind. Any time your feelings rise up to rule over your mind, you are in danger of disobedience because human feelings never take truth into consideration—they are rooted only in pleasure, not the consequences of pleasure. It is the *mind* that is capable of seeing the big picture, weighing consequences for actions, and determining right from wrong. Emotions see only the immediate gratification and the momentary pleasure. When you allow emotions to rule your life, you are suspending the judgment and reasoning of your mind. You are literally "out of your mind" when you let feelings dictate your behavior—you are "out" of your mind and "into" sensory perceptions, which include what you feel, taste, smell, touch, and hear.

The emotions do not recall God's Word or weigh the importance of God's commandments. Those are functions of the mind.

The emotions do not remember God's promises or God's warnings. Those are functions of the mind.

The emotions do not say "no" to things contrary to God's Word and "yes" to the leading of the Holy Spirit. Those are functions of the mind.

Putting the Spirit in Charge

Before you came to Christ, you did whatever popped into your mind. If you got an idea to do something, you did it. If you felt an urge or a deep feeling to act in a certain way, you acted on those urges and feelings.

Your spirit wasn't in control. Your mind and feelings were in control.

After you came to Christ Jesus, a different control mechanism entered your being—His name is the Holy Spirit. The Holy Spirit cleansed your heart and mind and gave you both the ability and the power to function according to a renewed *spirit*. You were made alive and new in the innermost part of your being—your spirit—and you were set on a path pointed toward a new spiritual destiny.

The command of God to you as a believer is, therefore, to rule your life according to the Spirit. In a very practical way, this means…

• **Renew your mind**. You are to know and live out the commandments of God and the principles of God found throughout the Bible. As you steep your mind and heart in the Word of God, the truth of God's Word begins to wash your mind and cleanse your thoughts so that what you think begins to line up with what God thinks, what you feel begins to line up with what God feels, what you desire begins to line up with what God desires, and, in the end, what you *do* begins to line up with what God desires for you to do, day in and day out.

God's Word says, *"Do not be conformed to this world, but be transformed by the renewing of your mind, that you may prove what the will of God is, that which is good and acceptable and perfect"* (Rom. 12:2).

The Holy Spirit brings God's Word to your remembrance at key moments in your life so you will know what is true and what is a lie, what is right and what is wrong, what is God's will and what is man's will. Jesus said, *"The Helper, the Holy Spirit, whom the Father will send in My name, He will teach you all things, and bring to your remembrance all that I said to you"* (John 14:26).

• **Walk in daily obedience to the Holy Spirit**. You must learn to listen closely for His voice as He directs you into making wise choices and decisions, and empowers you to respond to life's circumstances in a God-honoring way.

The Holy Spirit's ongoing work in our lives is to give us wise counsel and clear discernment. He says to us, "Trust Me. Listen to Me. I will lead you onto the path you should walk." And then, as we clearly discern His plan for us to follow, He says to us, "Trust Me. I will give you the power and provision and all the courage you need to live out this plan. Keep persevering in the way I am leading you, and I will make sure you experience an abundance of blessings and have an abiding sense of satisfaction, purpose, and joy."

• **Resist the devil's temptations to sin**. Before you came to Christ, you generally didn't think twice about whether something was sinful or not. You reacted to life in anger, wrath, malice, slander, and abusive speech. You lied freely to others, and to yourself. You didn't think anything of engaging in activities that you now know were immoral, impure, greedy, or rooted in evil desires and passions.

After you came to Christ, the Holy Spirit entered you and began to work on your conscience. He began to convict you in your spirit about what is ungodly and what is godly. The believer cannot sin "lightly" or "without regard." The believer is keenly aware that he has sinned, is sinning, or is about to sin. The Holy Spirit makes sure we *know* when we are facing a temptation to sin, and His word to us is always, "I will help you resist this. Trust Me. Count on Me to help you through this."

Renew your mind.

Walk in daily obedience to the Holy Spirit.

Resist the devil's temptations to sin.

That's the *life* each and every one of us has been given in Christ Jesus.

In putting the Spirit in charge of our lives, we are saying, "I choose to *think* and *act* differently."

This isn't just a matter of changing your mind about something. It's a matter of asking the Holy Spirit to change your mind so that you think in a completely different way.

The apostle Paul wrote to the Colossians:

Set your mind on the things above, not on the things that are on earth. For you have died and your life is hidden with Christ in God. When Christ, who is our life, is revealed, then you also will be revealed with Him in glory. Therefore consider the members of your earthly body as dead to immorality, impurity, passion, evil desire, and greed, which amounts to idolatry. For it is on account of these things that the wrath of God will come, and in them you also once walked, when you were living in them. But now you also, put them all aside: anger, wrath, malice, slander, and abusive speech from your mouth. Do not lie to one another, since you laid aside the old self with its evil practices, and have put on the new self who is being renewed to a true knowledge according to the image of the One who created him.

(Col. 3:2–10)

You Have to Guard How You Think

Even though we are made new in Christ Jesus, we are not immune from bad thinking or negative believing. We are not immune to taking in lies or operating in error. Our salvation is not some form of inoculation that protects a person from all forms of temptation, lies, deceit, or even the desire to sin.

Every believer is tempted—no matter how mature he or she becomes.

Every believer can buy into a lie—no matter how much he or she knows the Word of God.

Every believer is capable of sinning—no matter how long he or she has lived a pure life.

Every believer may make a mistake, make a bad decision or choice, or error—no matter how wise he or she has become.

We must *guard* our minds continually. We must persevere in reading and studying and applying God's Word. We must never think that we "have enough" of the Bible or that we "know it all." You can never exhaust all there is to learn spiritually.

If you are a true believer, you have the ability and the authority to take control over your mind. There have been times in my life when a thought has entered my mind and I literally have had to stop everything else I was doing and say, "Lord Jesus, I take authority over this thought! I ask You to drive this idea from my mind. I yield my life once again to the Holy Spirit and I ask You, Holy Spirit, to guard and protect me from every form of evil and assault from the devil."

And then, after you have taken authority over an ungodly thought in the name of Jesus, you must refuse to entertain that thought or allow your mind to return to it. Where so many people get in trouble is at this point—they begin to mull over the idea, dwell on it, fantasize about it, and allow it to lodge in their minds and emotions. You must say "no" to the idea and refuse to harbor it and nurture it.

"But how?" you ask. By willfully choosing to think about something else, and preferably, something that is about the Lord Jesus Christ! Start thinking about the Word of God that you read that morning—and if you haven't read the Word of God yet that day, pick up your Bible and start reading it aloud. Focus on it!

Think about what you are reading and how you can apply it to your life.

Start thinking about what the Lord has directed you to do in the way of ministry or church work—rehearse your part for the choir number next Sunday, start singing praise songs, open your mouth and give thanks to the Lord for all He has done for you and has promised to do for you today and in the future.

Think about the Sunday school lesson you are going to teach to the sixth graders next Sunday or the retreat that you are planning to help host next month or about whom you might recruit to help you with the ushering and parking responsibilities at church.

Think about ways in which you might bless your spouse or your children or your parents or a friend. What can you cook for dinner? How can you encourage that loved one in his or her work? What might you do to help that person with a need he or she may have? Get creative. Start thinking about new ways you might serve other people.

If you will take charge of your thinking and begin to focus your mind on something other than the thought you know is ungodly, sinful, unproductive, or totally fruitless, God will help you. He'll supply the power when you begin to exert your will to think in a godly direction! Before you know it, the ungodly thought will have vanished, and in its place you will have thoughts and attitudes and creative ideas that are worth acting upon, speaking out, and meditating upon! Those are ideas that can be turned into helpful deeds, acts of giving, and wise actions. And those behaviors on your part in their course will bring a blessing to your life!

Your blessing ultimately begins in your mind and heart every time. It begins with your taking control over your thought life, in the name of Jesus, by yielding your mind to the Holy Spirit. Your blessing is the outflow or the by-product of godly thoughts, godly attitudes, godly emotions, and godly actions.

The most potent thing you can think about, of course, is God's Word. That is where we will turn next, but before we do, I want to tell you about a young man named Sammy.

Sammy is retarded—at least that's the label that's been put on his life. He is mentally slow. But let me quickly assure you of this, there's nothing "slow" about Sammy emotionally or spiritually. Sammy lives out his faith, and he changes lives every day because of the way he lives.

Sammy has been an agent for helping countless people to "change their minds." He works in a very innocent, unassuming way. I'm not even sure he knows what he's doing or how he does what he does—he's effective anyway!

Sammy bags groceries at the local store. He hears a lot of comments about the weather as he carries out groceries. When people say to Sammy, "Wow, it sure is cold today," Sammy says, "Yep. We're going to have a fire in the fireplace tonight. I think Mom is going to fix hot chocolate. I like hot chocolate."

When people say to Sammy, "I wish it would rain," Sammy says, "Me, too. I like flowers and they need rain."

When people say to Sammy, "I hate this ice." Sammy says, "I like to watch the ice skaters on TV."

When he first picks up their groceries or takes over the cart, Sammy usually says to people, "I hope you are having a nice day. I am." It's hard for people to complain in response to a statement like that.

If a person grumbles or looks angry, Sammy is quick to say, "I like…" and then he'll find something to comment about. It might be "I like your tie" or "I like your mustache" or "I like your car." It's hard to stay angry when somebody as innocent as Sammy gives you a compliment.

I have absolutely no doubt that Sammy has a "renewed mind." He sees the good in life, the good in people, the good things in his own immediate future. He speaks what he sees. And I have no doubt that Sammy experiences what he thinks. He enjoys people. He enjoys hot chocolate on a cold night. He enjoys ice skaters and flowers.

What about you?

Are old thought patterns manipulating you in such a way that you are failing to enjoy your life? Isn't it time to break free from the negative thinking that is holding you captive?

A Prayer for Activating Renewal

I encourage you to pray today:

Father, free my mind. Free me to think Your thoughts. Free me to see the world as You see it.

I yield my mind to You today. Help me to set my thoughts on those things that are in keeping with Your will and Your plan for me. Help me to guard my mind against the temptations of the enemy.

I trust you to renew me today in my thinking.

In Jesus' name I pray. Amen.

4

The Power of God's Word

E very one of us faces the challenge of knowing the Word of God and making a commitment to live by it. God and His Word are inseparable. The Gospel of John opens with these words: *"In the beginning was the Word, and the Word was with God, and the Word was God"* (John 1:1). To know God is to have a hunger and thirst to know everything He has said to us. To know God's Word is to come to have an intimate fellowship with God. God's presence and power come to us and are quickened in us as we know and then live out His Word.

God's Word is mighty and powerful.

It is more powerful than the baggage of your past. It is more powerful than the way you were raised. It is more powerful than the messages of society about your life.

Most of us come to the Word of God after we have taken a great many other messages into our minds and hearts. Most of those messages were inaccurate, ungodly, or out-and-out lies.

The world's systems, the devil, and even the impulses of your own flesh cannot give you a message that is truly godly or accurate in the sense of your knowing the whole truth and nothing but the truth. The world, flesh, and devil operate according to lies, innuendos, misleading information, and error.

The devil is incapable of telling you the truth about God, about who you are as His creation, about how you can and must relate to God, or about how you can and must relate to other people. Jesus said very plainly that the devil is a liar and the father of all who lie. (See John 8:44.) The truth simply isn't part of the devil's nature.

The devil's messages to you will always be a variation on these themes:

• You are unlovable. God certainly can't and doesn't love you. Nobody else is likely to love you either.

• You are totally unworthy of a relationship with God. You don't have much value to Him or to anybody else.

• You may as well forget anything you've heard about God because you can never know Him. Live the way you want to live.

• You can never know with certainty what will happen to you after you die. But if there is life after death, surely you'll go to some place good. So follow whatever path you choose to follow, and believe whatever you want to believe.

• You don't need to follow any of God's commandments. You can live the way you want to live, and nothing bad will happen to you as a result.

The "fleshly" impulses you feel will not tell you the truth. The flesh says, "Satisfy me *now*. Do what feels good. Pleasure is the end result." That's never the *whole* truth, of course. The lustful desires of the flesh never tell about the aftermath of pleasure—the illness that may result, the pregnancy that may occur, the addiction that may develop, the guilt or shame or rejection or broken heart that is likely to be experienced.

The world simply reinforces what the devil and the flesh say. The world tells us to "tolerate" virtually everything, and "live and let live." The world holds to no absolute standards of truth, right and wrong, or good and evil. The world maintains that everything is relative.

God's Word stands in sharp contrast.

God's Word tells you the truth about yourself:

• God loves you.

• God values you highly.

• God desires to have a deep and abiding relationship with you.

• God wants to reveal to you a wonderful plan and purpose for your life. He wants you to fulfill the good destiny He planned for you even before your birth.

• God wants you to accept His Son Jesus as your Savior so you might live with Him in heaven forever.

• God has a way for you to live that will result in great eternal rewards and great earthly blessings. God's commandments are for your *benefit*.

The devil will tell you, "You're never going to get out of the trouble you are in today. You're always going to feel this bad."

The devil will ask you, "You don't feel loved by God, do you? Then why do you think you're loved if you don't *feel* loved?"

The devil knows if he can get hold of your affections—your thoughts and feelings—he will control your life, limit your destiny, and cut short your blessings.

The devil is relentless in his efforts to pull you back into a worldly mind-set. The pressure is always there to be distracted from the things of God and pulled back into compromise with the world and, ultimately, into sin. We face a daily challenge in putting the things of God *first*.

God's Word tells you the truth about the consequences of following lustful desires. God's Word tells you that this world operates ultimately according to God's absolutes. God is the sovereign King in charge of His universe. He does not tolerate sin. He has absolute standards for good and bad, evil and righteousness, morality and immorality. He judges and punishes sin, even as He rewards righteousness.

Make no mistake about it—the power of the truth is awesome. God's Word is truth. It is greater than any lie you have ever swallowed, either consciously or unconsciously. God's Word is more powerful than any bad teaching you have ever received, either by example, word, or in a formal instructional setting. God's Word is more powerful than any false conclusion you may have reached about yourself or God based upon what people have done to you, including the "use and abuse" you may have experienced in your past.

When you come to Christ, you are given a new beginning. You are made a *"new creature."* God's Word tells us, *"If any man is in Christ, he is a new creature; the old things passed away; behold, new things have come"* (2 Cor. 5:17).

God's Word says, *"The mind set on the flesh is death, but the mind set on the Spirit is life and peace"* (Rom. 8:6).

You are going to have to make a decision about that truth from God's Word. Either you believe it and choose to set your mind on the things of God, or you don't believe it—at which point, you are going to continue to think about, speak about, and participate in those things that are of the *"flesh."* The choice is yours.

The Word of God "Reprograms" You

It is the Word of God that "reprograms" our thinking. The Word tells us that Christ Jesus *"loved the church and gave Himself up for her, that He might sanctify her, having cleansed her by the washing of water with the word"* (Eph. 5:25–26).

We tend to have a bad connotation for the term "brainwashing." We associate it with coercion—with a person being forced to think differently. In truth, "brainwashing" can be a very positive thing. God's Word speaks of the Word "washing" our hearts and minds with truth. And the fact is, many people *need* to have their hearts and minds cleansed of lies, errors, and hurtful memories. They need to be cleansed of anger, bitterness, and hate. They need to be washed clean of leftover feelings associated with rejection or abuse.

Nothing "cleanses" our minds and hearts like the Word of God. Jesus said to His disciples, *"You are already clean because of the word which I have spoken to you"* (John 15:3).

God's Word always…

• **Bathes our minds with the *truth.*** It stands in sharp opposition to any lie we have been told by the devil about who we are, who God is, how God loves us and wants to build a relationship with us, and how God desires for us to be in loving relationships with other people. The truth is like a giant eraser for the mind—it wipes away the lies we have been told by the devil, the world, and even parents and others who may have inadvertently or willfully led us into error. In place of the lies, the Word plants in our minds and hearts the absolute assurance of God's love, His absolute commandments, and His absolute standards of right and wrong, good and evil, just and unjust.

The more we read God's Word, the more we begin to think as God thinks, feel what God feels, and know with certainty that we are children of God and people destined for a high calling in His kingdom.

• **Washes our minds and hearts with soothing, refreshing, cleansing *love.*** God's Word constantly points us to the mercy, forgiveness, and love of God. It reminds us again and again that God is for us, not against us—that God's desire is to bless us, protect us, preserve us, nourish us, nurture us, and provide for us *all* things that are for our eternal benefit. The more we experience God's love flowing over us, the easier it is for us to give up our feelings of hatred, anger, revenge, and bitterness. The more we hear and take into our hearts the Word of God, the more we feel God's presence, and the easier it is to rise up and say to ourselves, "God values me. He is with me. He will never reject me. He will never abandon me. He will never abuse me. He will *always* love me."

Any time you find yourself bathed in the *truth* and *love* of God, you are going to find yourself being healed and renewed. Things that are broken in you are going to be healed. Things that are out of alignment are going to be restored to alignment. Things that are missing are going to be "filled in" and provided. Things that have been uprooted are going to be replanted for fruitfulness. Things that have been ripped away from you or torn out of you or shredded inside you are going to be mended, replaced, and perfected.

A Continual Washing by the Word of God

How is it that we truly are "washed by the water of the Word"? (See Ephesians 5:26.) There are six things we must do, and do them continually.

1. We must read the Word daily. There is no substitute for reading your Bible on a daily basis—preferably first thing in the morning. Just as you must eat food daily to stay strong in your body, so you must partake of the spiritual food of the Word of God on a daily basis. Fill up your spirit with God's truth and God's love. Make it your *first* priority.

It takes discipline and a commitment to do your daily devotions *first* thing in the morning, to spend time in prayer *first* before going about your daily routine, to seek God's will *first* before you make major decisions.

God's promise to us, however, is that if we *"seek first His kingdom and His righteousness;...all these things shall be added"* to us (Matt. 6:33). He'll send us the relationships we need—He'll make it very clear to us without our scheming and manipulating or plotting and planning to "make" a relationship happen. He'll send us the material substance we need, without our groveling or demanding or whining about what we "think" we want—which so often turns out to be something that brings us no lasting joy. He'll send us the jobs and ministries He desires for us to do—He'll direct us in sovereign ways, providing all that we need, without our begging, coercing, or laying guilt trips on other people.

When we function out of our emotions, we nearly always end up using man-made methods to get what we hope will satisfy our emotional hunger. In sharp contrast, when we function out of a desire to seek what God wants and what God has promised, we find that we must rely on God-ordained methods—our faith, obedience, hope, love, and righteous living. In functioning out of a "hunger and thirst for righteousness" (see Matthew 5:6), we not only find that our emotional hunger is satisfied by the Lord, but also that He meets all the other longings and desires of our heart.

Let your "spirit man" dominate your "fleshly man."

If the devil can get a toehold on your mind and emotions—and begin to influence your thoughts and your fantasies and your imagination—he will soon control your behavior. If you allow him to continue to control your thoughts, feelings, and behavior, he will control your life and your destiny.

2. We must meditate on the Word. We are to meditate on the Word of God day and night—very simply, that means to think about God's Word almost continually. That takes tremendous discipline and focus! Oh, how easy it is to let our minds wander to that boyfriend or girlfriend we desire to have, that new possession we desire to acquire, that new enterprise we desire to undertake, and yes, even that new ministry we desire to launch. Our minds are quick to forget God's Word and pursue thoughts that serve only to gratify our emotions.

We must persevere in reading and studying and applying God's Word. We must never think that we have enough of the Bible or that we "know it all." You can never exhaust all there is to learn spiritually.

How do I know that to be true? Because God and His Word are inseparable. God is infinite. He is omniscient and omnipotent—you can never reach the end of knowing an infinite God, of experiencing all His power, or of learning all His wisdom. God's principles, His character, and His truth do not change—but His methods change continually. He never does anything in precisely the same way twice. His compassion, loving-kindness, and faithfulness are rock-solid certainties, but His mercies are new every morning. (See Lamentations 3:22–23.)

God's Word bears the same qualities. The truth of God's Word is so vast you can never fully take it all in. You can go back to a passage that you know well, and perhaps even have memorized, and find that God has a whole new level of meaning for you to take from that passage. The more you read and apply God's Word to your life, the more you realize that you will never exhaust all its riches. The principles, concepts, and commands of God in the Bible are absolutes. The comfort and truth and convicting power of the Word do not change. But the application of God's Word is as current as this morning's headlines. The ways in which God desires to work in your life are always in the "now"—His desire is always an immediate application to a very real circumstance, crisis, or situation in your life. God's Word is for "this relationship," and "that hang-up," "this appointment," and "that need." It is for "this choice," "that decision," this opportunity," and "that challenge." It is for "this attitude," "that belief," "this habit," and "that practice."

The Power of God's Word

The Bible tells us, *"All Scripture is inspired by God and profitable for teaching, for reproof, for correction, for training in righteousness; that the man of God may be adequate, equipped for every good work"* (2 Tim. 3:16–17).

I do not think I would be in error if I added four words to that verse: "in your life—today."

Notice that this passage tells us that all Scripture is *"profitable"*—it's for our blessing, our benefit, our good—today.

• All Scripture is inspired by God and profitable for *"teaching,"* in your life—today. God's Word clearly presents to you what is right and wrong, what is good and evil, what is essential for your blessing and what results in a curse.

• All Scripture is inspired by God and profitable for *"reproof,"* in your life—today. *To reprove* is to rebuke or convict. God's Word convicts us of our sin. It calls our attention to our own weaknesses, flaws, and faults—not so we will feel condemned, but so we will turn to God for forgiveness and for His strength as we seek to repent and change our ways.

• All Scripture is inspired by God and profitable for *"correction,"* in your life—today. God's Word clearly spells out *how* we are to turn from sin and walk in righteousness. It gives us the blueprint for how we might "mend and amend" our ways and live in right relationship with God and other people.

• All Scripture is inspired by God and profitable for *"training in righteousness,"* in your life—today. God's Word reveals to us God's ideals. It shows us the destiny we are to have in Christ Jesus. It shows us the pattern of what it means to be conformed to Christ's character.

What is the bottom line of these four main benefits from God's Word? That we might be *"adequate,"* which means that we might be fully prepared to face every problem, crisis, or need that comes our way. And that we might be *"equipped"* to do what God has called us to do.

The Word of God strengthens us, prepares us, equips us, warns us, and guides us day by day by day by day by day. The Word is for *now*—not ancient times, not even last week or yesterday. It is intended for immediate use and application in our own lives.

3. We must study the Word. Every Christian should be involved in some form of Bible study—not just once in a while, but continually. It may be a Sunday school or Bible study class you attend weekly; it may be Wednesday night Bible study at your church; it may be a study and prayer group you and your spouse attend together; it may be a series of tapes or a Bible study course that you are studying on your own. God's challenge to each one of us, no matter how mature we are in our faith, is to continue to explore the fullness of the depths of His Word. There's always something new for you to gain when it comes to the *truth* and *love* of God. There's always more insights to be gained.

4. We must memorize the Word. We must program God's Word into the memory banks of our minds so when the Holy Spirit desires to remind us of what God has promised or Jesus has said, the words of the Bible are readily present—we don't need to go look up a verse of Scripture that will give us comfort or guidance. The mind that is engaged in memorizing or recalling God's Word is *not* a mind that can be thinking about those things that bring about fear, doubt, worry, hate, revenge, bitterness, or anger.

If you are a parent, encourage your children to read and memorize God's Word with you. You'll be planting faith into your child's life that will produce good fruit. Even if your child rebels against the Lord, he or she will never be able to escape the truth of God's Word that has been engraved on his or her heart. Make memorizing God's Word a family activity—something you do on the way to school or as you run errands or as you stand in lines or sit in waiting rooms.

5. We must speak out or "confess" the Word with our lips.
Not only in crisis moments but as a routine part of our lives,
we need to be quoting God's Word to ourselves. As you read
the Bible in your daily devotional time, read it *aloud*. Your ears
will hear the Word, and the truth of Romans 10:17 will come
alive in your life: *"Faith comes from hearing, and hearing by the
word of Christ."* The spoken and heard Word—even if spoken
and heard by *you*—will cause your faith to become active and
energized.

Frequently speak aloud verses that you have memorized.
Reinforce the truth of God's promises and commandments to
your mind and heart. When you are faced with a major decision or problem, ask the Holy Spirit to give you guidance—
and then *speak* what the Holy Spirit brings to your mind.

Those who speak aloud the words of the Bible very often
experience great healing and restoration for their minds and
hearts. They find old hurtful emotions washed away by tears
that come as they "hear" God's expressions of tenderness and
love. They find their minds are able to function better—they
can concentrate, focus, and express themselves better—as a
result of their focusing on God's Word and reading it aloud to
their own ears.

Frequently speak God's Word to your children or your
Christian friends. Encourage those around you with words
of blessing from the Lord. You'll be encouraging yourself as
well!

6. We must accept the Word as being totally true for *us*. We
must choose to believe with our faith that *all* God's promises
are individually and personally for *us*, right now and in every
area of our lives. We must accept with our will that all God's
commandments are for *us*—we are each being called to obey
them and to discipline our lives according to them.

Look for ways in which to live out or to apply God's Word
to your life. If you seek to do this, God will be faithful in

showing you ways in which His Word applies. Time and again, I hear of people who read a passage of God's Word in the morning and before they go to bed that same night, God has given them an opportunity to share the truth of His Word with another person or has shown them a way in which the Word should be directly applied to their work, relationships, or personal life.

A woman said to me not long ago, "The scheduled reading on my Bible reading plan for last Tuesday morning was Psalm 18. We read the psalm for the day at the breakfast table before we pray. Then we each go off to work or school. That's our routine. Well, pastor, two verses of that psalm really stood out to me on that particular morning—verses two and three." She quoted these two verses to me:

The LORD is my rock and my fortress and my deliverer. My God, my rock, in whom I take refuge; my shield and the horn of my salvation, my stronghold. I call upon the LORD, who is worthy to be praised, and I am saved from my enemies.

Then this woman said, "At noon, I was having lunch with a friend at work and she told me that her former husband had started harassing her and calling her at all hours of the day and night. She no longer felt safe in her own home. I quoted these two verses from Psalm 18 to her and said, 'You've got to put your trust in God! You've done all you know to do—you've changed the locks on your apartment; you've had a restraining order issued against him. Start praising the Lord and trusting Him to be your refuge and your stronghold.' I prayed with this woman, and she told me that afternoon she was feeling much different in her spirit."

She went on, "About three o'clock that afternoon, I had a person come to me and tell me that a colleague in my office had started spreading lies about me. Like a flash, those two verses from Psalm 18 came to my mind and I said aloud,

'Praise You, Jesus! According to Your Word, when I call upon You, You will save me from my enemies. I praise You right now for being my Deliverer."

And still she went on, "When I went home that night, my teenaged son told me that a couple of boys at school had cornered him and demanded that he give them his lunch money. He said, 'Mom, I wasn't scared of them at all. You remember that psalm we read this morning? I stood my ground and said right out loud to those two guys, "Listen, the Lord is my Rock and my Fortress and my Deliverer. You can try to do anything you like to me, but let me tell you this, I've got a relationship with God and I'm trusting Him to deal with you. If that doesn't make you stop and think, it should." And you know what, Mom? They snarled a little and stared at me as if I'd completely lost it, and then they just turned and walked away.' I can't tell you, pastor, how happy that made me feel!"

Then this woman concluded, "Just in case you had any doubts, pastor, God's Word *works!* And it sure was working last Tuesday!"

Approach God's Word With Expectancy

As you read, meditate upon, study, speak, and believe God's Word, do so with great expectancy that the Bible is going to change your life! The more you rely upon God's Word, the wiser your decisions, the better your choices, the more godly your behavior, the stronger your faith, and the more loving your emotions will be. As a result, your relationships are going to be more enriching, and your work is going to be more rewarding. Your life *will* be transformed!

Shanika is living proof of this.

Shanika came to the Lord when she was in her early twenties. She had already lived what many would have considered a "lifetime" at that young age. She had left home when she was thirteen, lived on the streets, and worked as a prostitute for several years. Then, she found that she could make even more money dealing drugs to her sex customers. She not only sold drugs, but also used them. When she heard the Gospel of Jesus Christ, she could hardly believe that God would forgive her, that God loved her, or that God desired to be in relationship with her and restore her life to health and wholeness. The truth and love of God was almost more than she could take in. But Shanika gave her life to the Lord and began to attend church.

A Sunday school teacher in the church took Shanika under her wing, so to speak, and gave her a Bible that was easy to understand. Sometimes when she went to visit Shanika, Shanika would ask this teacher to read the Bible to her—she loved hearing the sound of the words of Jesus.

In many ways, Shanika's mind and heart had been fractured by the life she had lived. Her emotions had been shattered time and again. Her mind had been changed by the drugs she had used. Even her speech patterns had been affected by the drugs—she could hardly say a complete sentence or put together her thoughts to convey any kind of abstract idea.

This Sunday school teacher suggested to Shanika that she should read the Gospels out loud. She told her that if she didn't understand or couldn't seem to concentrate on what she was reading, she should read a passage again and again until she felt that God had spoken *something* to her. She said to her, "Shanika, read the words of Jesus out loud over and over until you can say, 'This is what Jesus is saying to *me*, to Shanika.' Repeat that truth to yourself all through the day."

Shanika, in very childlike faith and trust, began to do what the Sunday school teacher had said to do. She said not long ago, "When I look back, I can hardly believe the person I am today compared to the person I was back then. Some days, I could read only two or three verses before my mind felt tired.

But I'd read those two or three verses over and over. Sometimes I read them five or six times before I thought, 'Okay, that's what God is trying to say to me.' And then all day, I'd work very hard at remembering what I had read and what I knew God was saying. It seems like months that I did this. But then, I found that I was starting to read longer and longer passages. I started memorizing a few verses so I could quote them to myself. And the fact is, I still read my Bible out loud. I can concentrate better. I learn more."

An amazing healing took place in this young woman's life. When she came to the Lord, she was a bundle of hate and bitterness. She had been hurt so many times she had built a huge wall of self-defense in her soul. Over time, that wall began to crumble, and she found herself feeling love and compassion for other people. When this first happened, she went for months on the brink of tears—any display of tenderness toward her or any mention of God's love, and the tears would flow. Her Sunday school teacher told me, "I watched God wash away the crusted-on pain in her soul."

Gradually, Shanika's mind was also healed. She began to be able to think more clearly and to communicate more fully. She could concentrate better and focus on specific tasks. This, of course, allowed her to get a good job and to use the intelligence God had given her. She began to study God's Word. Before many months had passed, she was able to attend a Bible study and sit quietly and concentrate for up to an hour of study. That would have been impossible the year before—she would have been too fidgety and too unstable in her mind to sit and study *anything* for that length of time.

The more she studied God's Word, the faster and deeper the healing came in her life. Her life turned around in every area over the next two years. She met a man at her Bible study and began dating him. Eventually they married. She also began to help two other young women who came to accept

Jesus as their Savior and who had a background very similar to hers. She called herself their "big sister in Jesus." She began to read the Bible aloud to them, and over time, began her own Bible study to help them. She held them accountable for memorizing simple Bible verses that spoke of God's love, mercy, and forgiveness. Shanika also was promoted twice at her work, and eventually, she went back to get her high school diploma so she could get even more challenging and better-paying jobs.

If you saw this woman today—now nearly ten years after she came to the Lord—you would never dream that she had once led the life she led. You'd have no reason to even suspect she had ever been involved in prostitution or drugs. Because of the power of God's Word, she is a gracious, sane, sober, and godly woman, raising twin three-year-old boys.

What made the difference in this woman's life?

Oh, yes, she was genuinely saved and filled with God's Spirit. Yes, she had a good church home and stayed involved in it. Yes, she had a godly friend who encouraged her and taught her the Bible. But the one thing that truly made the difference in Shanika's life is that she allowed her mind and heart to be "washed by the Word." She read her Bible, studied it, memorized it, spoke it, and believed it. The truth and love of God came ringing from the pages of her Bible and healed her in her spirit, soul, and mind. The principles and promises of God's Word changed the way she felt and thought, and, in turn, renewed and transformed every aspect of her life.

What God's Word did in her life, it can do in your life!

A Prayer to Activate the Power of God's Word

I encourage you to pray today:

Father, teach me as I read Your Word today. Show me how You want me to think, feel, and respond to life.

Change the thought patterns of my mind to conform to Your Word. Let me speak and act on the basis of what You say. I want to ground my life on Your truth, Your commandments, Your principles, Your teachings, Your concepts.

I am trusting You to do what you have said You will do *according to Your Word.*

I pray this in Jesus' name. Amen.

5

The Power of Obedience

Maturity is all about doing things that you don't really want to do. Maturity involves a denial of many things you "want" in your natural, fleshly nature.

Maturity is saying, "I will eat vegetables even though I don't like them and don't want to eat them." Maturity is saying, "I will exercise every day even though I don't enjoy it."

Maturity is saying, "I may be attracted to you, baby, but I have to stay away from you because you aren't a godly person or you aren't available, and therefore, you aren't for me."

Maturity is saying, "I will go to church next Wednesday night even though I'm tired."

Maturity is saying, "I will tithe even though I'd rather spend my money on that new 'bauble' or 'toy' I saw at the mall or the local car dealership."

Maturity is about discipline. It is about obedience.

Maturity in Thoughts and Feelings

Maturity is not only to be manifested in our behavior. It is also a word that is to apply to our emotions and our attitudes. Maturity is saying, "I will not live by my emotions." Maturity is saying, "I will not give in to prejudice or hate or anger."

Just as you are required by God to take charge of your *thinking*—to line up your thinking and believing according to the Word of God instead of according to what the devil whispers in your ear, what your flesh urges in your body, or what the world sets out as a standard—so God requires that you take charge of your *feelings*. It is up to each one of us to take charge of our emotions and to rule over them, rather than allow them to rule over us.

Obedience Runs Contrary to the Flesh

Obedience is an act of your will—just as faith, forgiveness, and a renewal of your mind according to God's Word are as well. It runs contrary to the flesh and to emotions.

If you allow your emotions to rule your life...

You will always "react" to people instead of responding to them with clear, godly words and behavior.

You will always be suspicious of other people because you feel they are equally suspicious of you.

You will always give in to your prejudices.

You will be quick to take revenge or strike out in anger.

You will struggle to think positively about your life and your future.

Emotions run high—but they also can run very low. A person can be filled with elation one minute and be in the pit of despair the next. Emotions are fickle. They change from moment to moment, circumstance to circumstance.

Obedience to the Lord, which comes from our *will*, is a force that can produce steady, constant, and faithful behavior. Our will is the seat of our ability to make a commitment and keep it, our ability to endure and persevere in speaking and doing what we know is right and godly, our courage and boldness in speaking out against what we know is wrong or evil, our faithfulness in serving the Lord regardless of what others around us are doing.

When we are obedient to the Lord, we are no less emotional. By this, I mean that we continue to feel the full range of emotions given to us by God. But rather than have our emotions jerking us about, first one way and then the next, our emotions are focused, and they drive us to take godly action and pursue pure, godly goals.

Let me give you an example of this.

Renata was a woman I knew many years ago who lived out of her emotions. She had a sister Marva. People who only casually knew these two sisters sometimes labeled them "hot" and "cold"—they saw Renata as a woman of great passion while Marva came across to them as a woman who was a little cold, aloof, and standoffish.

What people discovered when they got to know these two sisters better was that as high, happy, and passionate as Renata could be at times, she was also prone to depression, despair, great fear, and lashing out when things didn't go her way. She felt her emotions to the extreme, and they ruled her life. If a man treated her well, she was on top of the world. If things didn't go her way, or if she felt that someone was mistreating her, she could be abusive in her language, and, at times, she was quick to pick up the nearest heavy object and throw it at a person she felt had done her wrong. Afterward, she'd feel remorse, but she rarely if ever apologized. She had dark periods she called the "blahs" when she didn't want to be around people.

Now, Renata was a Christian—don't misunderstand me on that point. She had accepted Jesus as her Savior, and she was doing her best to follow Him as the Lord of her life. But in many ways, her emotions dictated her spiritual life. If she liked the music or felt the power of God during a revival, she was quick to praise and to cry and to laugh and to be very demonstrative in her worship. If she was hurting or in a "blah" period, however, she'd usually stay away from church and if she did attend, she tended to be critical of everything from the choir to the sermon.

Emotions ruled Renata. She didn't rule her emotions or allow the Holy Spirit to rule her emotions.

Marva also knew the Lord. Granted, she was of a slightly different temperament than her sister—a little more serious and a little more industrious. But mostly, Marva made a decision early in her Christian walk that she was going to submit her entire life to the Lord, including her emotions.

In truth, Marva didn't feel any *less* deeply about various circumstances and situations than her more volatile sister. But Marva took a different approach. When she felt joy, she turned that joy into acts of giving. She took her joy to the local nursing home and gave away her joy in the form of hugs and bouquets of flowers and spontaneous "concerts" around the piano in the lobby of the nursing home.

When Marva felt sorrow, she wept, but then she turned to others to comfort them. She didn't withdraw from people— she reached out to them. In times of sadness, she turned to the Lord and to the church, not away from fellowship with God and His people.

When Marva felt angry at an injustice, she used that anger as fuel to speak out against the injustice or to take positive action to remedy the circumstances that gave rise to the negative situation. For example, when she discovered that the poor children in the neighborhood day care center were being kept from swimming lessons because they didn't have enough money to pay for them, she went to the day care center leaders and voiced her concern. She asked for permission to approach people in the name of the school to ask for contributions to give "swim scholarships" for the needy children. She took action out of her anger, and she saw results from her positive actions. It took her only five phone calls, by the way, to raise the money needed so all the children could learn to swim.

When Marva felt fear, she didn't frantically run to every person she knew to get help—as Renata was prone to do. Rather, she fell on her knees and cried out to God for help. If she turned to anybody else, it was to the women in the Bible study she attended to ask them to pray for her.

What happened to these two women over time?

Renata turned to alcohol as a means of dealing with her "blahs." She has struggled with alcoholism for nearly twenty years—most of the time sober but, on occasion, she has also abused alcohol to the point of needing to be hospitalized. She has been through three marriages, and her current marriage also seems on the brink of divorce. The men she married couldn't handle her continual emotional roller coaster. One of the men once said to me, "I was worn out after just two years of living with her. Everything was a crisis or done at fever pitch. Nothing about our life together was stable or consistent. One day we were on top of the world and no love had ever been finer—the next day she was just sure we were headed for divorce court and no relationship had ever been as troubled. I never knew where I stood with her. It was as if I was living on an earthquake fault."

Marva, on the other hand, has been married to the same man for twenty-two years. They've raised two children who have finished high school and junior college and are employed in their community. Both of her children love the Lord and are involved in church. Marva has been the head of a church ministry outreach to the homeless—a ministry that provides blankets, gloves, hats, sweaters, and coats to those in need of these items. She is a person whom others turn to for comfort, counsel, and wise leadership. Her husband said to me not long ago, "People know they can count on Marva, and the fact is, the children and I have counted on her more than we know. She's our rock."

Now, do Renata and Marva both feel—do they each have emotional responses to life's circumstances? Absolutely. Marva doesn't feel any less or have any less emotion to her than Renata. Do they have different ways of expressing their emotions? Yes.

But a difference in *expressing* emotions is not what truly makes the difference in these two women's lives. The real difference is this: Renata is ruled by her emotions. At any given moment, the enemy of her soul is able to pull her emotional strings and cause her to jump away from God and toward sin. Marva rules her emotions, with the help of the Holy Spirit. The devil has no ability to "jerk her about." Marva turns her emotions over to her *will*, which has been yielded to the Holy Spirit, and the result is that her emotions drive her to take action that is productive and beneficial.

Let me emphasize this process of yielding our emotions to our will.

Emotions are related to *sensory perceptions.*

Your will is related to your ability *to choose and to decide.* Your will is also related to your ability *to make a commitment* and *to stand by it.*

If you make choices strictly according to your feelings, without your will being actively engaged, you are likely to choose whatever is most convenient, pleasurable, and, in most cases, self-serving. Your choices and decisions are likely to be quick, "in the heat of the moment" decisions—they may be right and good decisions, but there's also a significant likelihood those decisions and choices may be bad ones.

As Christians, we are called to submit our will to the Holy Spirit—at all times, in all situations, about all things, and in all relationships. We are to say continually as Jesus said, "Not my will, but Your will be done in my life." (See Luke 22:42.)

This means that when we feel a surge of emotion—either good or bad, from fear and anxiety to happiness and peace—we are to say to the Lord, "What would You have me do? How shall I respond? What shall I say?"

Your will, yielded to the Holy Spirit, then becomes a driving force for whatever it is that the Holy Spirit directs you to do.

Emotions by themselves are like gasoline. A little match brought too close to the fumes can result in an explosion. Your will is like the engine of a car. Put that gasoline into the tank of the car and it can be used for a good purpose without an explosion. Furthermore, if you yield your will to the Holy Spirit—who would be the driver of the car in this illustration—then your car is going to go where He directs it. It will be used to haul what He wants hauled, provide transportation for those He wants transported, and take you to places where He wants you to serve and worship!

Your emotions may very well tell you to "speak your mind" to another person. Your will, yielded to the Holy Spirit, will direct you to "speak God's Word" to that person.

Your emotions may very well tell you to "strike out" at someone who has hurt you or criticized you. Your will, yielded to the Holy Spirit, will direct you to "reach out" to that person who has caused you pain—perhaps reaching out in an act of kindness, or in the spiritual realm with an act of prayer.

Your emotions may very well tell you to "have sex" with that person who is not your spouse. Your will, yielded to the Holy Spirit, will direct you to "build a God-centered relationship" with that person.

And, in the end, which is the most productive, beneficial, rewarding, and satisfying result? You may feel a moment of emotional "release" in speaking your mind, striking back, or having sex; but, in the end, you are likely to feel miserable, guilty, and sorrowful that you took those actions. The more productive, beneficial, rewarding, and satisfying results are going to come as you speak God's Word, reach out in prayer and kindness, and build relationships that are God-authorized, and therefore, God-blessed.

As long as you live strictly by your feelings, you will not receive the fullness of all that God has promised to you.

As long as you live by your feelings, you will be calling folks you shouldn't be calling, you'll be stopping by houses you shouldn't be stopping by, you'll be doing things you shouldn't be doing.

As long as you live by your feelings, you'll be having sex with people you shouldn't be having sex with, you'll be hanging out with people you shouldn't be hanging out with, you'll be disobeying God in all sorts of ways you shouldn't even be *thinking* about!

As I shared in the previous chapter, the apostle Paul wrote, "*Set your mind on the things above, not on the things that are on earth*" (Col. 3:2). In another translation of the Bible, this verse says, "*Set your affection on things above, not on things on the earth*" (KJV). Paul was referring to the emotional bent of your heart—those things you dwell upon in your desires, those things you think about because they are rooted first in your emotions and your "wants."

What Is Required by Obedience?

Obedience requires two main things of us:

- We put God first in all things.
- We keep God's commandments with joy.

Putting God First

Obedience goes beyond the letter of the law. Obedience means following the "spirit" of the law—which is to love God with all one's heart, soul, and mind. Obedience means putting God first in all things.

Never forget that the first of the Ten Commandments is this: *"I am the LORD your God....You shall have no other gods before Me"* (Exod. 20:2–3).

God not only deserves the number one position in our lives—He requires that we give Him the number one position.

Who or what are you putting before God today?

The truth is, every person becomes a slave, or a servant, to whatever he puts first in his life. If you put the pursuit of wealth as your first priority, you will become a slave to your job. You will become a servant to the almighty dollar rather than a servant to the almighty God. You will "worship" the possession of things and the acquisition of property and other forms of material wealth.

If you put the pursuit of fame as your top priority, you will become a slave to the masses. You will become a servant of your "fans," always doing what they want you to do and always striving to be what they want you to be, rather than doing what God wants you to do and seeking to become who God wants you to be.

If you put the pursuit of power as your top priority, you will become a slave to any organization or method that you perceive gives you authority or rule over others. You will pursue any avenue that you perceive leads to your having greater "control" over others, and you will make that pursuit with such a slavish drive that you will lose all compassion for the weak and the innocent. You will also lose out on all the joy associated with being in a giving-and-receiving relationship with other people.

In sharp contrast, if you put God first, you will pursue the things of God as your first priority. You will want to do what is right in God's eyes. You will want to be there when the church doors are opened for a service. You will want to become involved in church activities and church outreach ministries. You will want to give. You will want to pray and read your Bible and be part of a Bible-study class and a prayer group. You will want to live a godly life in your home and on your job and in your community.

God's promise is that if you put Him first, He will direct your steps and provide for you fully—just as an ancient landowner in Bible times provided for His servants.

Keeping the Commandments with Joy

Many people know they are supposed to "keep God's commandments"—in other words, obey the law of God. But Jesus went beyond that. He linked keeping His commandments with our receiving and manifesting *joy*. Jesus said to His followers,

> *If you abide in Me, and My words abide in you, ask whatever you wish, and it shall be done for you. By this is My Father glorified, that you bear much fruit, and so prove to be My disciples....If you keep My commandments, you will abide in My love; just as I have kept My Father's commandments, and abide in His love. These things I have spoken to you,* ***that My joy may be in you, and that your joy may be made full.*** *This is My commandment, that you love one another, just as I have loved you.*
> (John 15:7–8, 10–12; emphasis added)

If you are not experiencing joy today, ask yourself, "Where am I missing it in my relationship with God? What commandment of the Lord am I not obeying?"

Your joy is directly tied to Jesus Christ. Jesus is your joy. He is your love, your peace, your very reason for being. Every character trait of Jesus is a character trait that the Holy Spirit desires to build into your life in an abiding, lasting way. God's Word lists for us the traits that you and I are to have as Christians: "love, joy, peace, patience, kindness, goodness, faithfulness, gentleness, and self-control." (See Galatians 5:22–23.) Any time we are not experiencing an overflow of one of these traits in our lives, we can draw one very simple conclusion: We don't have enough of Jesus in us. Our relationship with Jesus in some way has become weak or damaged.

What does the most to damage our joy? Sin.

And just as the Bible lists those traits that are ours when our relationship with Jesus is strong and healthy, so the Bible lists *sins* that damage our relationship with Jesus and cause us to become less loving, less peaceful, less patient, less faithful, less gentle, and to demonstrate less goodness and be more out of control. Those sins, called *"the deeds of the flesh"* (Gal. 5:19), include immorality, impurity, sensuality, idolatry, sorcery, enmities, strife, jealousy, outbursts of anger, disputes, dissensions, factions, envying, drunkenness, carousing, and *"things like these"* (v. 21). God's Word says plainly, *"those who practice such things shall not inherit the kingdom of God"* (v. 21).

Did any of the words in that list of sins cause you to feel a pang of guilt? If so, that was the Holy Spirit expressing grief or sorrow over your sin. Pay attention to that guilt! Do something about it!

Go to God and admit to Him that you aren't living the way you know you *ought* to be living. Confess to Him that you aren't speaking or acting in a way that brings glory to His name. Admit that you have been pursuing a lifestyle or the purchase of possessions or a position of power that is not in keeping with His commandments or His purpose for your life.

Ask God to forgive you! Don't delay in this.

What did Jesus command?

Jesus commanded us to love our enemies and to live free of any spirit of revenge (Matt. 5:38–48).

Jesus commanded us to treat other people as we want to be treated (Matt. 7:12).

Jesus commanded us not to worry but to seek first the kingdom of God and His righteousness (Matt. 6:33–34).

The New Testament is filled with Christ's commandments about how we are to live in relationship to God and other people. Read those commandments, and then heed them.

A continual breaking of God's commandments will result in your grieving the Holy Spirit. You will not have joy. The commandments of God—and obedience as a whole—will become a drudgery and a burden to you. On the other hand, a keeping of God's commandments gives freedom for the Holy Spirit to work in you, through you, and all around you. You *will* have joy. And the commandments of God—and obedience as a whole—will not be a burden, but a delight.

Obedience and Your Love of God

God's Word tells us,

Whoever believes that Jesus is born of God; and whoever loves the Father loves the child born of Him. By this we know that we love the children of God, when we love God and observe His commandments. For this is the love of God, that we keep His commandments; and His commandments are not burdensome. For whatever is born of God overcomes the world; and this is the victory that has overcome the world—our faith. And who is the one who overcomes the world, but he who believes that Jesus is the Son of God?
(1 John 5:1–5)

Those who are truly born again have a desire to obey God's commandments. Even if your flesh says otherwise, you desire to do what God wants. You may fail from time to time, but your motivation, your intent, your heart's longing is to obey God.

God's Word tells us in this passage that the keeping of God's commandments is not a "burden" to us—it isn't hard. How can this be?

Because we know that God loves us and His commandments are ultimately for our benefit and blessing.

Jesus taught, *"Take My yoke upon you, and learn from Me, for I am gentle and humble in heart; and* YOU SHALL FIND REST FOR YOUR SOULS. *For My yoke is easy, and My load is light"* (Matt. 11:29–30). The yoke refers to learning and doing His commandments— carrying out our daily responsibilities in such a way that we reflect Jesus to the world. How can bearing such a yoke be *"easy"*? How can bearing a yoke bring *"rest"* to the soul? Consider these two main reasons—the best yokes are those made so that each side is carved individually for each ox. Such a yoke fits *perfectly.* The yoke that Jesus puts on us is designed to fit us as Christians. His yoke fits who we are as a new creation—it fits our identity as Spirit-filled and Spirit-led believers. Second, oxen work in teams. You aren't under the yoke by yourself. The Holy Spirit is in the yoke with you. He's pulling with you. He's walking with you. He's working inside you, alongside you, and all around you. God's Word assures you that you have the power of the Holy Spirit dwelling inside you and *"greater is He who is in you than he who is in the world"* (1 John 4:4). We are empowered and enabled by the Holy Spirit to keep the commandments.

The Lord will never tell us to do something that is not good for us. His commandments keep us out of trouble and bring healing to our souls.

When a person comes to Christ, it isn't hard for that person to give up drugs because that person knows what drugs did to his or her life. When a person comes to Christ, it isn't hard to give up drinking because a believer has a new awareness of what alcohol did to his life. When a person comes to Christ, it isn't hard to give up adultery because a believer has a new awareness of what infidelity does to a marriage and a family.

Jesus also said, *"Blessed are those who hunger and thirst for righteousness, for they shall be satisfied"* (Matt. 5:6).

The normal hunger and thirst of a person's heart is for those things that will satisfy the flesh. It is a driving force that flows from a person's emotions—a desire for things that bring satisfaction, pleasure, immediate gratification, sensual delight, or sexual release. It is a driving force that pursues all things that might build up a person's esteem, feelings of power, and feelings of self-worth—including the acquisition of things, status, and "stuff" that becomes the envy of others. These drives and desires that flow from man's emotional state are very powerful, just as powerful as the physical desires for food and water when a person is extremely hungry or thirsty.

Jesus said, "Hunger and thirst for the things that put you in right standing with God. Desire those things that are godly and that build you up spiritually. If you pursue those things, you truly will be *'satisfied.'*" This word *"satisfied"* means fulfilled, with a feeling of wholeness and purpose and deep abiding peace and joy. It means to be at rest so that you aren't always craving or seeking something because of a deep inner lack, want, or need you have.

If you pursue what God says is good for you, He'll provide for you all things that are truly good for you. He *will* set you free from the devil who is trying to rule your life. He will free you from all that is enslaving you.

Your commitment to obey God in all things is vital for your breaking free and then living free!

A Prayer to Activate Obedience

I encourage you to pray today:

Father, I want to obey You. Help me to obey You fully, in all things, every day, in all ways, in all relationships, in all encounters I have, in all the work I do, in all the words I speak.

Help me to live my life in such a way that I am not ruled by emotions, but by obedience to Your Word.

I pray this in Jesus' name. Amen.

PART II

Living Free

In these next chapters, I want to cover ten of the most damaging emotional states I have encountered in my years as a pastor and bishop. These emotional strongholds are ones that truly keep us tied to Satan himself, who attempts to manipulate and control our lives against everything God's Word says and our own faith says. If you feel yourself emotionally "hung up" today, it is very likely because you are struggling with one of the following:

- Guilt
- Nagging Negativity
- Fear
- Bitterness
- Depression
- A Victim Mind-Set
- Failure in Relationships
- Jealousy
- A Spirit of Failure
- Past Sins and Habits

Today is your day to break free, and then *live* free. God's will for you is not that you be in bondage, but that you walk boldly, freely, and confidently as a witness of Christ Jesus your Savior and Lord!

LIVING FREE

6

Moving beyond Guilt

A woman once said to me, "I know what guilt sounds like."

I replied, "You do?" I have had countless people tell me they know what guilt *feels* like, but I had never heard someone say he or she knew what guilt *sounded* like.

"Yes," she said very seriously. "It sounds like the lid of the porcelain cookie jar slipping from your fingers while you are stealing a forbidden cookie. It makes just enough noise that you know with certainty that Mom heard it all the way back in her bedroom."

For many people, guilt is not just a momentary zinger of conscience or a feeling of getting caught doing something you shouldn't be doing. For many people, guilt is a constant state of misery because they *know* with certainty that they have done something that deserves punishment.

Guilt says, "I know I have done wrong and that I should be punished for it." If guilt remains unresolved in your life for long enough, you will walk in shame and a degree of depression, which will set you up for failure the rest of your days.

One of the most powerful passages of the Bible about guilt is found in the book of Revelation:

I heard a loud voice in heaven, saying, "Now the salvation, and the power, and the kingdom of our God and the authority of His Christ have come, for the accuser of our brethren has been thrown down, who accuses them before our God day and night. And they overcame him because of the blood of the Lamb and because of the word of their testimony, and they did not love their life even to death." (Rev. 12:10–11)

Note that in this passage of Scripture, the accuser—the devil—is described as the accuser of *"the brethren." "The brethren"* is a reference to believers, those who are "saved," committed Christians.

The devil doesn't need to waste his time accusing sinners. They don't feel guilt the way a believer feels guilt. In fact, most people who are deeply mired in their sin have long ago justified it as something that everybody does, something they can't help doing, or something they do because "God made them that way." Guilt for most sinners is buried deep within, and it is truly the sovereign work of the Holy Spirit to remove the blinders from their spiritual eyes so they can see their sin for what it is and desire to have it removed. It is the work of the Holy Spirit—through the Word of God and the love of Christ—to reach into the soul and cause people to desire the forgiveness of God. Then they can experience peace and a freedom from guilt once it is brought to the surface where it must be confronted and dealt with.

Even after you have accepted Jesus Christ as your Savior, the devil will come to you to try to accuse you of your past wrongdoings. His effort regarding guilt and shame is against those who have been forgiven. Why? Because if the devil can convince you that you deserve to feel guilty and ashamed, you will think, feel, and respond to life as if you have never been forgiven. You will have to contend with shackles still around your soul, and your life will be far less effective for Christ Jesus, and far less successful. This occurs even though the chains have been unlocked and you can cast them off and walk in freedom. The person who continues to feel guilty long after he or she has been forgiven by God is a person who thinks of himself, at least to some degree, as still being a sinner and a failure. And as a person thinks, so he or she will speak and act.

Have you ever seen an elephant tied up outside a circus tent? Usually the elephant is secured to its position by a fairly small chain attached to a peg that has been driven into the ground. How is it that such an insignificant peg and chain can hold back such a big animal? This happens because the elephant was first tethered to the ground as a young animal. It learned as a baby elephant that it had limits in its mobility. Even when the elephant became fully grown, that early conditioning was still there. The fact is, a full-grown elephant could easily pull up the peg and chain restraining it, but it stays in place because it doesn't *know* it could roam just about any place it chose to roam. It *thinks* it is being held in place, and so it is held in place.

This is exactly the way guilt operates in the lives of a forgiven person. The person has been conditioned to think of himself as guilty, ashamed, and in some way diminished in value. Even after he is forgiven, he continues to think in old patterns. And the result is that in many ways he is just as shackled by his former sin as if he had never been forgiven!

Guilt will give you a "why try?" attitude. It will rob you of any joy you have in serving the Lord because you see yourself as being unworthy, undeserving, and unqualified to receive any good thing from God's hand.

The guilty person does not use his faith to believe God for the fullness of God's blessings.

The guilty person will not walk in forgiveness, will not make an effort to start over, and will not believe that it is

93

possible to go on in life and experience any degree of success.

The truth of God is always...

You can be forgiven!

You can start over!

You can go on!

Overcoming Feelings of Guilt

How does God's Word say we overcome the accusations of the devil against our lives? How do we overcome guilt related to our past lives or our most recent sins?

Two things are required: the blood of the Lamb, and the word of our testimony.

1. The Shed Blood of Jesus. The blood of the Lamb, of course, refers to the crucifixion of Jesus on the cross. It is because Jesus died for our sins and became the atoning sacrifice for them that we are able to be forgiven. He is the Lamb who laid down His life so that we might be saved. God's Word says to us: *"You were not redeemed with perishable things like silver or gold from your futile way of life inherited from your forefathers, but with precious blood, as of a lamb unblemished and spotless, the blood of Christ"* (1 Pet. 1:18–19).

There's no way you can "give" your way out of guilt, do enough good works to cover over your guilt, or attend enough church services and sing enough choir numbers to wipe away your guilt. The only way you can deal with guilt is to accept the fact that Jesus Christ died for your sins and that when He says you are forgiven, you are forgiven. The Bible declares to us, *"The blood of Jesus His Son cleanses us from all sin"* (1 John 1:7).

You must see yourself as being forgiven. You must accept and receive what Jesus did on the cross as being for you.

When the time came for the children of Israel to be released from Egypt, God told Moses to have each family of the Israelites take an unblemished lamb and kill it at twilight. Then, they were to sprinkle some of the blood of that sacrificed animal on the two door posts and on the lintel of the houses in which they were going to eat of the lamb after it had been roasted. (See Exodus 12:1–13.) The Lord said, *"When I see the blood I will pass over you, and no plague will befall you to destroy you when I strike the land of Egypt"* (v. 13).

Nobody could point to the blood on somebody else's house and say, "That applies to me, too." In like manner, every one of us must say, "What Jesus did on the cross applies to *me*." It doesn't matter if your grandfather was a preacher, your aunt is a saint of the church, your sister is the choir director, or your brother is the head usher. It doesn't matter if every person in your family tree is born again. It doesn't matter if your family built the church building and donated the cross over the altar. What matters is what *you* believe about Jesus dying on the cross and what *you* do about receiving Him as *your* Savior.

The blood of Jesus is more powerful than any "death agent" that comes against your life. Jesus said that His shed blood and your *belief* in His sacrifice brings you eternal life. Death is defeated! Any sin that comes to attempt to cut short your life, your witness, your blessing, and your destiny is a sin that is under the blood of Jesus. That sin has no power to kill God's work in you.

There's an old gospel song that has as its chorus, "There is power, power, wonder-working power in the blood of the Lamb. There is power, power, wonder-working power in the precious blood of the Lamb!"

From cover to cover, the Bible declares that life is in the blood—and even more so, *eternal* life and all things that make for an *abundant* life on this earth are in the blood of Jesus that He shed on our behalf!

Begin to see that shed blood of Jesus as flowing over your entire life!

Actively Receive God's Forgiveness

You must actively, intentionally, and consciously *receive* God's forgiveness into your life. The fact is, you have been forgiven! The fact is also that unless you *believe you have been forgiven* and begin to speak and act *as if you are forgiven*, you will continue to be emotionally tied up in things God desires you to be free from! You will be unable to move beyond yesterday's pain.

God's Word tells us, *"If we confess our sins, He is faithful and righteous to forgive us our sins and to cleanse us from all unrighteousness"* (1 John 1:9). This verse doesn't say, "some of the time" God is faithful to forgive us. And it doesn't say that He will cleanse us only from "some forms of unrighteousness." The truth of God's Word is that He *always* forgives us when we come to Him and say, "Heavenly Father, I have sinned. I'm sorry. Please forgive me. Please help me to turn away from this sin and never go back to it again." The truth of God's Word is that He always forgives us and cleanses us from *all* unrighteousness. He wipes it from our hearts, our lives, and from His own memory.

The same is true for any sin you commit after you are saved. Your forgiveness lies in your *receiving God's forgiveness* and then living in that forgiveness. God's Word says,

> *If any man is in Christ, he is a new creature; the old things passed away; behold, new things have come. Now all these things are from God, who reconciled us to Himself through Christ, and gave us the ministry of reconciliation, namely, that God was in Christ reconciling the world to Himself, not counting their trespasses against them, and He has committed to us the word of reconciliation.* (2 Cor. 5:17–19)

The truth of God is that when you accept Jesus Christ as your Savior, you *are* saved, you *are* transformed into a new creature, and you *are* forgiven. The truth of God is that any time you yield to temptation and sin, from that point on, God stands ready to forgive you the moment you come to Him, confess your sin, ask for His forgiveness, and ask for His help so that you truly might repent—turn away from your sin and toward godly living.

God never runs out of forgiveness for you as a believer. He always stands ready to forgive you and to help you repent as you put your trust in Him.

I mentioned earlier in this chapter that guilt comes when we believe we should be punished for something we have done. When you are certain that Jesus has been punished for your wrong, and you gratefully accept that He took your punishment in your place, then you must walk out of your guilt into freedom and joy! It is a choice you make based upon the shed blood of the Lamb.

2. The Word of Your Testimony. The second thing we must do is guard very carefully the words of our mouth. We overcome guilt in part by the word of our testimony.

If you continue to say to others, "I'm just a sinner" or "I'm a dirty ol' dog that'll never get clean" or "I'm a failure in God's eyes and I'll always be a failure," that's the way you are going to live your life! You will not be free of your guilt!

On the other hand, if you say to others, "I'm a forgiven child of God" and "I'm in the process of being refined just as fine silver and gold are purified" and "I'm being transformed day by day into the likeness of Christ Jesus," that's the way you are going to live your life! You will be free of guilt. You will experience the joy of the Lord. You will want to use your faith. You will want to live a godly life. And you will move forward into God's fullness of blessing!

What you say is very important. It doesn't bring about your salvation, but it does seal the truth of your salvation to your mind and heart!

We each face the tremendous challenge of trading the devil's lies for God's truth when it comes to guilt.

The devil says, "You're a sinner."

Now, the truth of God is that every person has committed sin in his life prior to accepting Jesus as Savior. No person comes to Jesus Christ as a sinless person. We all have things in the past we wish we hadn't done, said, thought, or felt. We all have things we wish we could do over in a better or more godly manner. The Bible tells us, *"All have sinned and fall short of the glory of God"* (Rom. 3:23). Furthermore, God's Word says, *"If we say that we have no sin, we are deceiving ourselves, and the truth is not in us....If we say that we have not sinned, we make Him a liar, and His word is not in us"* (1 John 1:8, 10).

Yes, we *are* sinners. But the devil has left out a very important word in his lie. The truth is, each one of us who has accepted Jesus Christ is a *saved* sinner.

The devil says to us, "If you were *really* saved, you wouldn't have done that. If you were *truly* born again, you wouldn't be feeling or thinking or speaking or acting this way." He comes to lay a guilt trip on us.

If we give the devil a toehold with this line of argument, he will move right on to remind us of who we once were—and he'll attempt to convince us that "nothing has changed." He'll tell us that we are just as much a sinner as we ever were, that Christianity doesn't work, that forgiveness from God is a myth, and that we are totally undeserving of salvation, eternal life, and the abundance of God's blessings.

Lies, lies, lies.

The devil will tell you, "You've sinned too many times." God's truth is, you can never sin too many times to be forgiven.

The devil will tell you, "You've worn out God's patience, committing this same sin again and again." God's truth is, every time you come to Him for forgiveness, He will forgive you.

The devil will tell you, "That sin is a whopper. It's too big for God to ever forgive or forget." God's truth is, there's no sin too great for His forgiveness.

What you say back to the devil is part of your "testimony."

When the devil comes to lay a load of guilt on you, you need to speak right back to him, "Devil, I may not be perfect yet. But I'm being *perfected* by God. I'm God's child. I have received the shed blood of Jesus as being on my behalf. I believe Jesus is my Savior. My heart's desire is to follow Jesus as my Lord. I have confessed my sin to God and He has forgiven me. I will not receive a load of guilt from you because as far as God and I are concerned, I have been *cleansed* completely of my sin. And furthermore, I'm trusting God to help me walk in such a way that I won't yield to your temptation again."

Start declaring to yourself, "I am forgiven."

Start declaring, "I am the righteousness of God."

Start declaring, "I am cleansed of *all* unrighteousness!"

Regardless of How You Feel

"But," you may be saying, "I don't *feel* forgiven." God's Word tells us that *"we walk by faith, not by sight"* (2 Cor. 5:7)—and certainly not by our feelings.

Your salvation has absolutely nothing to do with the way you *feel*. It has nothing to do with anything you *do* in an effort to earn your salvation. It has nothing to do with anything you *say* in some form of ritualistic reciting of dogma. Your salvation is all about what *Jesus* did, not what you do.

Jesus died on the cross for you. He died so you might be forgiven of your sins and receive the gift of eternal life. He died so you might be restored to a right relationship with your heavenly Father, be filled with the Holy Spirit, and receive the fullness of an abundant life on this earth. That's what Jesus *did*.

Your part is to believe and receive. It is to accept, by your faith, that Jesus is who He said He is, that Jesus did what He did, and that Jesus will be true to what He promises. Your part is to receive Him as your Savior and to make a commitment with your will to live your life in a way that is pleasing to God and in keeping with His commandments.

There's not one ounce of feeling required for you to be saved or for you to be forgiven.

Whether you feel anything or not, you are to live your life according to what God's Word says.

I don't keep the Ten Commandments because I *feel* like keeping them. I keep them because God's Word says to do it.

I don't give my tithes and offerings to God because I *feel* like giving. I do it because God's Word says to do it.

I don't forgive those who hurt me because I *feel* like forgiving them. I forgive because God's Word says to do it.

I don't walk free of guilt because I *feel* like I'm guilt-free. I walk free of guilt because God's Word says that I'm free of guilt!

Conviction and Guilt Are Very Different

Conviction and guilt are not the same thing.

Conviction draws you toward God and toward His forgiveness. When, as a believer, you fail God and sin, you feel "conviction"—which is an awareness that you have sinned. Your first impulse, then, should be to run toward God and cry out for mercy and forgiveness. The Holy Spirit's desire in convicting you is that you will turn from your sin, turn toward God, receive forgiveness, and then walk in a way that is opposite of your sin!

Guilt causes you to want to run and hide from God—to move as far away from Him as possible because you fear His punishment. Guilt is not something the Holy Spirit imparts to you. It's something that comes from your *believing* the devil's lies and drawing your own false conclusions about God and His ability to forgive.

The believer who buys into guilt is saying, in essence, "God's ability to forgive isn't absolute. It's limited. It's conditional. It doesn't apply to all my life, all the time." The believer who accepts the accusations of the devil and allows them to dominate his mind and heart is saying, in essence, "What the devil says to me is more true than what God says to me."

Guilty people don't go to church—they stay away from church. They don't want the preacher, the Sunday school teacher, or even the person sitting next to them in the pew to even suspect they are as a guilty as they feel they are!

Guilty people don't seek out godly friends—they stay away from godly friends and seek out people they think are just as guilty as they are.

Guilty people don't run to the altar to repent—they run as far away as possible.

Guilty people act like Adam and Eve in the Garden of Eden when they knew they had sinned and were deserving of punishment. Adam and Eve *"hid themselves"* (Gen. 3:8), or so they thought. They tried to keep God from finding them. It didn't work then, and it doesn't work now.

God knows exactly where you are. You may fool a lot of people, but you aren't fooling yourself, and you certainly aren't fooling God. If you have sinned, He knows it. But His desire is not that you feel guilty, but rather that you come to Him and say, "I have sinned. I need your forgiveness. I believe in what Jesus did for me, and I accept His blood as covering that sin. Please forgive me on the basis of what *Jesus* did, not on the basis of what I have or haven't done. Please cleanse me and help me from this moment on."

Women who have had an abortion...

People who have divorced a spouse...

Men who have fathered a child and then abandoned that child, whether unborn or born...

And those who have committed adultery...

Seem especially prone to guilt even after they are saved. They just can't seem to forgive themselves for what they have done.

God's Word says, *"There is therefore now no condemnation for those who are in Christ Jesus. For the law of the Spirit of life in Christ Jesus has set you free from the law of sin and of death"* (Rom. 8:1–2).

You are going to have to make a decision about that truth from God's Word. Either you believe it, or you don't.

Judas betrayed Jesus to the temple authorities. Was he guilty of being disloyal to the Lord? Yes. Did he feel guilt? Yes. Did he turn from that guilt and receive Jesus' forgiveness? No, he threw himself off a cliff in self-judgment and killed himself.

Three times, Peter denied knowing Jesus. Was he guilty of being disloyal to the Lord? Yes. Did he feel guilt? Yes. Did he turn from that guilt and receive Jesus' forgiveness? Yes, and he went on to be a leader in the church after Jesus ascended into heaven.

Are you guilty of being disloyal to the Lord? In some way, at some time, yes, you are. None of us is ever 100 percent loyal to the Lord. Do we feel guilty when we don't live up to the life we know God has for us to live? Yes.

The real question is, What are you going to do with the guilt you feel? Are you going to run to Jesus to receive His forgiveness, to renew your commitment to Him, and to receive His help as you go down life's road? Or are you going to live in self-condemnation, fall away from the Lord, and, in the end, destroy the potential for your life of blessings?

Could Judas have been forgiven? Absolutely. If he had only sought out Jesus to confess and repent of his sin, Jesus would have forgiven him in the same way He forgave Peter. Judas could have gone on to complete the ministry he had been chosen to accomplish in his life. Can you imagine the power of his witness? He would have had to be able to say, "I am the chief of all sinners, but God forgave me. If Jesus could forgive me, surely He can and will forgive you!" But Judas cut all that short. He condemned himself by not asking Jesus to forgive him.

Jesus said very plainly, *"Do not condemn, and you will not be condemned"* (Luke 6:37). Jesus wasn't speaking only about condemning other people. He was also speaking about our condemning ourselves. If we condemn ourselves, we will not go to God for forgiveness, and the result is that we will not be forgiven, and therefore, end up condemned! On the other hand, if we refuse to condemn ourselves and run to Jesus for forgiveness, He freely and fully forgives us, and we are not condemned! The choice is ours.

This doesn't just pertain to our salvation.

We are condemning ourselves any time we say, "I'm not good enough." It's saying, "I'll never amount to anything." It's saying, "I'm a failure and always will be one."

If we condemn ourselves in these ways, we will not go to the Lord and say, "Help me! Help me to receive Your love. Help me to dream Your dreams and begin to desire what You want me to desire. Help me to succeed in the ways You desire for me to succeed!" If we condemn ourselves and fail to go to Jesus for help, we won't receive His help, and, in the end, we will fall short of all He desires for us.

On the other hand, if we refuse to condemn ourselves and go to the Lord and cry out to Him for His help, wisdom, counsel, understanding, direction, power, provision, and protection, He'll give us those things we ask for with our faith! He'll answer our cry, and we will receive those things we need. As we receive His help and apply His wisdom and strength to our lives, in the end, we will receive all He desires for us!

The choice is ours. Any time we condemn ourselves in any way, we are refusing to seek God's help and forgiveness, and we will fall short of the fullness of who God created us to be. Any time we refuse to condemn ourselves and turn to God for help and forgiveness, we are moving ever closer to being and doing all God created us to be and do!

Ask God to Give You a Testimony

If you don't see a "before and after" story in your life, ask God to reveal to you what your life truly was like before you came to call Him Savior. Or if you accepted Jesus at a very early age, ask Him to show you what your life *might* have been like had you not come to Him when you did. The fact is, we each have a before and after story in our lives.

Melvin was a man who knew he had a "before" story. Guilt nearly kept him from believing for an "after" part to his life story.

Melvin got involved with the wrong crowd and dropped out of high school. He had been raised by a godly grandmother, but when he got involved with the wrong crowd, he also rebelled against everything his grandmother had taught him about Jesus and the Bible. He dropped out of church at the same time he dropped out of school. He told anybody who asked, and mostly he told himself, that he wanted nothing to do with his grandma's God.

Through the years that followed, Mel went from one petty crime to another, mostly being a pickpocket and committing home burglaries. Sometimes he worked with a partner; sometimes he went it alone.

At his grandmother's funeral, Mel heard the Gospel for the first time in about a dozen years. What he heard convicted him. He felt a sense of wrongdoing that he hadn't felt in years, and, at the same time, he felt an overpowering sense of God's love and desire to forgive him. The next Sunday evening, Mel went to church and at the close of the service when the invitation was given to accept Christ Jesus, Mel nearly ran to the altar. He received God's forgiveness.

But then he faced the biggest struggle of his life—forgiving himself and *walking* in forgiveness. Mel continued to see himself as a thief. He wondered about every person he met, "Is this somebody that I stole from?" He carried a trainload of guilt.

Fortunately for Mel, when he came to Christ, he was assigned a spiritual friend at the church. This friend refused to give up on Mel. He sought him out. He helped him get a job. He invited him to a Bible study. When Mel didn't show up at church or Sunday school, this friend went looking for him.

One day, this friend had a talk with Mel, and Mel said to him, "Listen, I'm a hopeless case. I've sinned too many times to have all my sin washed away. I'd like to be forgiven, but I don't feel forgiven. I still feel like a dirty sinner."

His friend said, "You say you are hopeless, but God says you aren't hopeless, and I say you aren't hopeless. God and I are two against your one. You're outnumbered." He told Mel he would be coming to his house the next night to *prove* to him that he and God were right.

The next night, this friend showed up on Mel's doorstep with twenty people from the church. They walked in with gifts of food for Mel's pantry and other items they knew would bless him in his life, including a couple of easy-to-read books on forgiveness and living free of guilt and shame. Mel was overwhelmed when he saw this large group of people outside his door. He began to weep, and in those tears he cried, the guilt washed away from his soul.

Every person in that group said to Mel that night, "Mel, God loves you, and I love you. God says you are worthy, and I say you are worthy. God says He forgives you, and I say you are forgiven. God says you must not walk in guilt, and I say you must not walk in guilt."

And then, these people laid their hands on Mel and prayed for him that he would live free of guilt and shame and, very specifically, that the Holy Spirit would empower him to walk in boldness, confidence, peace, and joy.

That night changed Mel's life.

It's now twenty-two years later. Mel is the janitor at a church. He also works as a night janitor for several small businesses owned by church people. For more than two decades, this church and these businessmen and women have trusted Mel to clean their places of business. They have given him access to all kinds of things that, in his former life, Mel might have stolen. Nothing has ever shown up missing. Mel is no longer a thief. He's a man with a witness. He's a man who says, "I once was a sinner. Now I'm saved. I once was lost. Now I'm found."

What made the difference? It was the shed blood of Jesus. And it was the word of the testimony of loving Christian brothers and sisters. Ultimately, it was the word of Mel's own testimony, staring at himself in the mirror and proclaiming, "I am not the man I once was. Jesus has changed me. I'm a new person in Christ."

What are you saying to yourself today?

What are you saying to others who may be walking in guilt or shame?

Most important, what are you believing about the blood of Jesus? What is your testimony about what He has done for you?

7

Moving beyond
Nagging Negativity

Have you ever met a person who is always negative?
Have you ever known a person who always believes the
worst about any given situation, person, organization,
or possibility?

Negative attitudes, thoughts, and words produce negative
results.

God says to us, "I am positive, and the relationship I desire
with you is *positive*." God is all about positives.

After creating every aspect of the natural world, God said,
"It is good." After creating mankind, He said, "It is good."
(See Genesis 1.) The work that God does today is 100 percent
totally good. Everything He touches, He touches with blessing,
goodness, and an abundance of life.

The prophet Jeremiah gave this word from the Lord: *"For
I know the plans that I have for you,...plans for welfare and not
for calamity to give you a future and a hope"* (Jer. 29:11). That
word *"welfare"* in this verse does not mean what we have come
to know as welfare in our world today. Welfare referred to all
that would make a person "fare well"—it was a word related
to great blessing, wholeness, and goodness. God promised His

people all the goodness they needed and all the protection from calamity that they needed, so they would have *"a future and a hope."* God intends for your future to be *better* than your past. He intends for your hopes to be in something *good*, rather than an expectation of something negative.

Jesus said, *"The thief* [the devil] *comes only to steal, and kill, and destroy; I came that they might have life, and might have it abundantly"* (John 10:10). An abundance refers to an overflow of vitality, energy, health, material provision, and blessing. God's desire is that His people not only have their needs met but that they have an "overflow" they can give to others.

David said about the Lord,

He drew me out of many waters [dangers].

(2 Sam. 22:17)

He delivered me from my strong enemy, from those who hated me. (v. 18)

He also brought me forth into a broad place [of goodness and influence]. (v. 20)

The LORD has rewarded me. (v. 21)

He makes my feet like hinds' feet, and sets me on my high places. (v. 34)

David knew that everything good in his life had come from God—his life had been *preserved* by God, his position as king had been *secured* by God, and his future was *assured* by God.

Are you trusting God today to preserve you? Are you trusting God to be your security? Are you looking to God as the Source of your confidence?

David declared,

*Thou hast also given me the shield of Thy salvation, and
Thy help makes me great. Thou dost enlarge my steps under
me, and my feet have not slipped.* (2 Sam. 22:36–37)

God's Word tells us, *"Every good thing bestowed and every
perfect gift is from above, coming down from the Father of lights,
with whom there is no variation, or shifting shadow"* (James 1:17).
God's goodness doesn't change. Goodness is His very nature—
lasting and sure. *Everything* He does for us, in us, and through
us is good.

Therefore…

If everything that God has to say about you is good,

If everything that God does toward you is for your ultimate good,

If everything that God gives to you is good,

Isn't it time that you started lining up your thinking,
believing, speaking, and acting to reflect God's positives?

Everything Is Ultimately under God's Control

Not only is everything God does and plans *good,* but everything is ultimately under His control.

People seem to gravitate to one of these two negative positions in a time of crisis or trouble:

• God has given up on me.
• God couldn't do anything about this.

Neither one of those positions is true according to God's
Word.

The truth is, God never gives up on His people. He
may have allowed a problem to arise in your life for the
purpose of chastening you, disciplining you, refining you,
or strengthening your faith. His purpose in allowing that
problem is ultimately for your good. He wants you to be

purified, strengthened, and conformed to the likeness of Jesus Christ. He hasn't given up on you—He believes in you enough to want to see you changed, transformed, renewed, and put into position for an even greater blessing in your life!

The truth is, God never loses control. He is always in charge of every aspect of His creation. No problem is too great for Him to solve. No question is too tough for Him to answer. No situation is too difficult for Him to resolve. There isn't *any* type of affliction that is too great for God to deal with, heal, defeat, or deliver you from. God's Word says, *"Many are the afflictions of the righteous; but the LORD delivers him out of them all"* (Ps. 34:19).

Jesus said, *"In the world you have tribulation, but take courage; I have overcome the world"* (John 16:33).

No matter what you are facing today, God has not forgotten you, He has not neglected you, He has not forsaken you, and He has not given up on you.

No matter what you are facing today, God is in control of every area of your life. He has a plan for your growth, your renewal, and your future. Everything about His purposes toward you is good.

You Have to Choose the Positive Path

You are not automatically set free from all negative feelings, thoughts, or attitudes the moment you are saved. In many cases, those feelings, thoughts, and attitudes will continue to come to you—usually when you least expect them and do not desire them!

When the children of Israel were finally set free by Pharaoh, they began marching toward the land that God had promised to them. But it was only a matter of days before Pharaoh sent his armies to pursue the children of Israel, with the goal of bringing them back into captivity.

I assure you, the devil will attempt the very same thing in your life. He doesn't want to see you enter the fullness of all that God has promised for you. He doesn't want you to be totally set free from his bondage. He wants you to continue to serve him in sin, including sinful thoughts, feelings, and attitudes.

Time and again, I talk to people who tell me that a particular "sin" of their past has risen up with its ugly serpent head and has tried to snare them once again. Sinful people try to regain their ability to influence a believer to sin. Sinful behaviors try to entrap the believer once again. Sinful thoughts creep in and try to gain hold.

What God promises to us is that as we continue to trust Him and cry out to Him, He will keep our past from ever totally overwhelming us again. From God's perspective, the sin of our past is *in our past*.

Oh, Pharaoh's armies did their best to chase down the Israelites and overwhelm them. But, in the end, God opened up the Red Sea, His people marched across it on dry ground, their lives were spared, and God allowed the soldiers, horses, and chariots of Pharaoh to drown in the Red Sea as the waters came crashing back upon them.

Trust God to do that delivering work in your life. Trust Him to put down His foot and to put out His everlasting arm to say "no" to the devil's pursuit of you.

This deliverance of your mind and emotions doesn't happen automatically. You must cry out to God for it. You must trust God for it. You must receive this deliverance into your life and refuse to look back over your shoulder at sin. Instead, you must walk forward with your faith toward all that God has for you.

Three Things You Must Come to Know

There are three vital truths of God's Word that you must come to know if you are going to be set free and live free from nagging negativity:

111

You must know who you are in Christ.

You must know your "rights" as a child of God.

You must know the promises of God to you.

1. Know Who You Are in Christ. Every person has a *degree* of low self-esteem. In some way, every person has self-doubts and an awareness of his or her own faults, flaws, and weaknesses.

The way we all overcome low self-esteem is the same whether we have very low self-esteem or fairly high self-esteem. The challenge we each face is to determine who we are in Christ Jesus.

What does the Bible say about you?

Who does God say you are?

When you truly understand who you are in Christ Jesus, it isn't going to matter what other people say about you, what other people seem to think or feel about you, or how other people treat you. The only thing that will matter to you is whether you are doing what the Lord has said about you, how He feels about you, and whether He is pleased or displeased with what you say and do.

Show me a genuinely confident, bold Christian man or woman and I'll show you someone who *knows...*

• that God loves with an unconditional love.

• that God is merciful and forgiving.

• that God is at work in transforming every believer into the likeness of Christ Jesus.

• that God is patient, kind, and good—*all* the time.

• that God is the giver only of good gifts and that God has given unique talents and abilities to every person.

• that God provides for every need, both now and in the future.

• that God protects every believer from the devil's assaults and gives strength to overcome every type of temptation.

• that God can be trusted in every situation to be a loving Father.

Sin No Longer "Fits"

As you come to know who you are in Christ, you will soon discover that sin simply doesn't "fit" your identity anymore. God's Word declares:

> *Do you not know that all of us who have been baptized into Christ Jesus have been baptized into His death? Therefore we have been buried with Him through baptism into death, in order that as Christ was raised from the dead through the glory of the Father, so we too might walk in newness of life. For if we have become united with Him in the likeness of His death, certainly we shall be also in the likeness of His resurrection, knowing this, that our old self was crucified with Him, that our body of sin might be done away with, that we should no longer be slaves to sin.* (Rom. 6:3–6)

Jesus made it very clear that our sin is not limited to what we do. Sin begins with the attitudes and emotions of our hearts. When our attitudes and emotions are out of line with God's desires, they give rise to sinful words and deeds.

Jesus said, *"For out of the heart come evil thoughts, murders, adulteries, fornications, thefts, false witness, slanders. These are the things which defile the man"* (Matt. 15:19–20).

In other words, every act of murder begins with an attitude and emotions that are "murderous" in their intent. Every act of sexual sin, every theft, every verbal sin against another person begins with a wrong attitude and emotion.

Sinful thoughts and attitudes no longer "fit" us as believers in Christ Jesus.

Anxiety and Worry No Longer "Fit"

God's Word tells us, *"Be anxious for nothing"* (Phil. 4:6). Therefore, anxiety no longer "fits" our identity as believers in Christ Jesus.

It's time for you to face up to the truth that...

There are some things you can change, and some things you cannot change.

There are some things you can fix, and some things you cannot fix.

Not everybody is going to love you or want to live in peace with you, no matter how much you love them or want to live in peace with them.

There are a million things that can cause you to worry, but only one Lord who can take care of every need, problem, crisis, or difficulty you face. Focus on the One you can count on, rather than on the million things you cannot control.

God calls us to do what we can do—and to do *all* that we can do—given the capabilities and direction He has given to us. Then, we are to trust what we do, and all that we cannot do, to His care. We are to leave the consequences of our best efforts up to God.

God's Word says, *"Humble yourselves, therefore, under the mighty hand of God, that He may exalt you at the proper time, casting all your anxiety upon Him, because He cares for you"* (1 Pet. 5:6–7).

Don't feel as if you have to *make* your own success happen. Recognize that the timing of your reward and your recognition by others is in God's hands. The harvest of your blessing is according to His timetable.

God's Word tells us,

Let us not lose heart in doing good, for in due time we shall reap if we do not grow weary. So then, while we have opportunity, let us do good to all men, and especially to those who are of the household of the faith. (Gal. 6:9–10)

He who sows sparingly shall also reap sparingly, and he who sows bountifully shall also reap bountifully. Let each one do just as he has purposed in his heart; not grudgingly or under compulsion; for God loves a cheerful giver. And God is able to make all grace abound to you, that always having all sufficiency in everything, you may have an abundance for every good deed. (2 Cor. 9:6–8)

Do all that is within your power to love others, obey God's commandments, and minister to the needs of others, and then rest in the full assurance that you have done what God requires of you. Trust Him to reward you in His timing.

Fear and Doubt No Longer "Fit"

Two of the greatest weapons in the devil's arsenal against your mind are fear and doubt. Let me be even more precise regarding these emotions—they are *nagging* fears and *nagging* doubts. Certain momentary, passing, natural fears and doubts are normal to life. The persistent, nagging, and binding fears and doubts are the ones that no longer fit our identity as believers in Christ Jesus.

God's Word is very clear about the identity we are to take on in Christ. One of the main statements that you will read throughout the Bible is this: "Fear not!" God knows that one of the devil's foremost tactics is fear. As you read God's Word, you are going to find yourself reading, "Fear not! Fear not!" again and again. This phrase is in the Bible dozens of times. Eventually, you are going to have to conclude: "Either God means this or He doesn't. I have a choice to make. I can choose to be fearful, or I can choose to trust Him." And when you make that choice to rely upon God's strength, your fear will always begin to subside.

One of the foremost commands in the New Testament is, "Believe." You are going to find it more than a dozen times in the Gospel of John alone. God knows that one of the devil's favorite tactics is doubt. As you read God's Word, you are going to find yourself reading again and again, "Believe, believe, only believe." Eventually, you are going to have to come to a decision: "Either God means for me to use my faith or He doesn't. I must choose to *believe*." And when you make that choice to believe God's Word, your doubts will begin to recede.

Know Your "Rights" as a Believer in Christ Jesus

As a believer in Christ Jesus, you no longer have certain rights.

Just because you have been hurt does not give you any right to act in a foolish or ungodly manner.

Just because somebody else said something about you does not give you the privilege of responding with hate, anger, gossip, or slander against that person.

Just because you were treated unfairly does not give you any license to lash out at another person or group of people.

No Right to a Trouble-Free Life

You also have no right to a trouble-free life. There is nothing in the Word of God that ever promises you that you will be spared all heartache or trouble in your life. In fact, if you are a believer in Christ Jesus and you are living a godly life, you can expect a certain amount of persecution and trouble solely *because* you are living for God. God doesn't promise us roses without thorns, but God does promise us that He will walk through every step of our lives with us. He will be there in every moment of heartache, every moment of sorrow or sickness or tragedy or crisis, every moment of persecution or misunderstanding or criticism or rejection. He will never leave us or forsake us. He will help us and provide for us and bring us through those trying times with victory and joy in our hearts. He will use those difficult times to make us stronger in our faith, wiser in our decisions and choices, more energized in our faith, and bolder in our witness.

No, you do not have a "right" as a believer to a trouble-free life. None of us lives in a "fair" society. But we do serve a just God. If we will do what God tells us to do, He will make certain that we receive justice even when society doesn't provide justice to us. You do, however, have the right to go immediately into God's presence, to cry out to the Lord for help, to yield all your thinking and feeling to the Lord, and to receive His guidance and help. You do have a right to pray and to intercede and to speak the Word of God to your negative situation. You do have a right to act courageously and boldly and in a godly manner, even if everyone around you is encouraging you to take revenge, retaliate, or react in anger.

No Right to Hate

You also have no right to hate another person. You only have a right to show kindness and to love others, including your enemies.

Do not tell me you love God if you hate a person because he or she has a different skin color than yours.

Do not tell me you love God if you hate your mother-in-law, or your daughter-in-law.

Do not tell me you love God if you hate your former spouse.

Do not tell me you love God if you hate your former boss or a former coworker or your troublesome neighbor.

I'm not saying those people don't *deserve* to be hated. I'm telling you that you have no *right* to hate them.

God's Word is very clear on this point. It tells us, *"Whoever does not practice righteousness is not of God, nor is he who does not love his brother"* (1 John 3:10 NKJV).

God's Word also instructs us,

By this we know love, because He laid down His life for us. And we also ought to lay down our lives for the brethren.
(v. 6 NKJV)

Let us love one another, for love is of God; and everyone who loves is born of God and knows God. He who does not love does not know God, for God is love.
(1 John 4:7–8 NKJV)

If someone says, "I love God," and hates his brother, he is a liar; for he who does not love his brother whom he has seen, how can he love God whom he has not seen? And this commandment we have from Him: that he who loves God must love his brother also.
(v. 20–21 NKJV)

No Right to Anger or Revenge

God's Word says very clearly,

Never pay back evil for evil to anyone....If possible, so far as it depends on you, be at peace with all men. Never take your own revenge.
(Rom. 12:17–19)

What is it that causes a person to feel deep anger? One of the core reasons for anger is that our pride has been wounded. We didn't get the promotion we thought we deserved. We didn't get the respect we thought we should receive. We weren't treated with dignity. We weren't recognized in the way we thought we ought to be recognized.

Every one of us is selfish to some degree—all the way from the person who has a strong survival instinct to the person who is a totally self-absorbed, me-first, I'm-number-one egomaniac.

When we don't get what we want, we get mad.

Now, what we want may actually be what we need or what we rightfully believe is owed to us. When we don't have basic needs met in our lives, we tend to get angry at those who deprive us of what we need. When we don't get what we rightfully believe is owed to us, we get angry at those who seem to have denied us our basic human "rights."

But let me ask you this: Who truly can meet *all* your needs? Let me assure you, no person or institution or organization of any type—no matter how great, how generous, or how good—can *ever* meet *all* your needs. Human beings, and organizations made up of human beings, are fallible. They make mistakes. They fall short. They disappoint us.

The truth is that only God can meet all your needs, all the time.

If you aren't getting what you think you need or what you believe is rightfully yours, go to God with the matter. Don't get mad at other people who have failed you. Take your hurt feelings and your wounded pride to God!

This holds true for every negative emotion. Ask yourself...

"Why am I feeling so angry? Why do I erupt from time to time in negative, angry outbursts?"

"Why am I feeling so jealous that I resort to telling lies about others or spreading gossip that will undermine the success of others?"

"Why am I feeling so great a need to control a situation or to control other people—to the point that I am continually clamoring to have my way?"

"Why am I feeling so bitter, to the point that I want others to suffer and feel as bad as I do?"

Own up to the negative emotions you are feeling, and ask God to cleanse you of these emotions. Ask Him to forgive you for what you have said or done that has in any way hurt or discouraged another person. Ask Him to forgive you for what you may have said or done that has caused another person's reputation to be damaged.

Make a decision to seek God's forgiveness for any emotion that is not in keeping with the character of Christ Jesus, and you will be taking a giant step toward freeing yourself from depression and putting yourself into position to experience the joy of the Lord.

So many people launch out in prayer against the person, group, or organization they believe has caused them pain or injury. That's not at all what the Word of God teaches. The Word of God instructs us to *"resist the devil"* (James 4:7). When we do, it promises that *"he will flee"* (v. 7). We are to stand strong in prayer, fully "clothed" or "armed" with the identity of Jesus Christ. (See Ephesians 6:10–18.) And, as a part of our prayer life, we are to pray for God to work in the lives of those who have trespassed against us—sinned against us, hurt us, spoken out against us, or in any other way trampled on our lives. We are to do good to the ones who have hurt us. By praying and doing good, we put ourselves into position to receive God's rewards back to us. His justice, His provision, His "making it right" are the result of our yielding to Him and doing as He directs.

Your Only Real Right

The only real "right" you have as a believer is the right to yield your mind, heart, and total life to the Holy Spirit; as He directs you to pray and respond, you can then use the name of Jesus to come against the devil who inspired that person or group to hurt you, speak against you, or treat you unfairly. I encourage you to read that sentence again. The only right you have as a believer is to yield your life to the Lord and know that each and every time you do, He will direct you, guard you, provide for you, and reward you. He will lead you in the path you should go. Usually that is going to be a path of prayer and a path of positive, godly action. He will lead you to rebuke the devil in His name and to pray for a blessing on the person who hurt you!

2. Know What God Promises You. There are three main things that God promises to you: His peace, His joy, and His abiding presence.

His Peace

Jesus said, *"Peace I leave with you; My peace I give to you; not as the world gives, do I give to you. Let not your heart be troubled, nor let it be fearful"* (John 14:27).

Peace is a word that appears frequently in the Bible. Again and again, you will find references that speak to the God of peace and the peace that Jesus gives. You will be confronted over and over with commandments to cast all your care upon the Lord. Eventually you will come to the crossroads: "Either I'm going to receive God's peace, or I'm going to continue to feel anxious. The choice is up to me." And when you choose to receive God's peace, as promised in His Word, your anxiety will dissolve. Strength and boldness and confidence will replace the worry you once felt.

God's Word offers God's presence and power in place of fear.

God's Word offers truth and faith to replace doubt.

God's Word promises peace and strength in place of worry and anxiety.

The more you saturate your mind with God's Word, the less place you will give to fear, doubt, and worry.

Any time you feel an attack from the enemy, which strikes fear in your heart, cry out to God. Begin to speak His Word aloud. Fear *will* go.

Any time you find yourself struggling with doubts, go to God. Ask Him to give you His answers. Begin to read your Bible. Doubts *will* go.

Any time you feel overwhelmed with anxiety, panic, or worry, say, "Lord, help me. Give me Your peace!" Just as He spoke peace to calm the storm, He'll speak peace to the storms in your life. He'll remind you of the way He has provided for you or protected you in the past. As these thoughts fill your mind, His peace will reign in your heart. Anxiety and worry *will* leave you.

The truth is...

There are very few things worth losing sleep over.

There are even fewer things worth hanging on to from day to day.

There is *nothing* worth losing your family over, losing your peace over, or going to hell over!

It's a waste of your time and energy to continue to dwell on what your parents did to you, what your former friend did to you, or what an unfair employer or teacher or coworker did to you.

It's over!

His Joy

God also promises to give us joy as we follow and obey Him.

Now, many people confuse happiness and joy. When they don't feel happy every moment of the day, they automatically assume that something is wrong. Their minds turn to all kinds of negative thoughts, such as, "Something's missing in my life," "I'm not satisfied," "God must not love me," "I must be a failure," "I'm not getting what I need."

If these thoughts are allowed to go unchecked, they can lead to deep dissatisfaction with life and increasing discouragement and despair. Depression isn't far away.

Don't confuse joy with happiness.

Possessions can make you happy—until the "new" wears off that toy or bauble.

A new boyfriend or girlfriend can make you happy—until you really get to know that person.

Circumstances and situations can make you happy—until rain falls on your parade.

Joy is deep, lasting, and abiding. It is rooted in an assurance that you are in right relationship with God and God is in charge of every aspect of your life; therefore, all things ultimately are going to work for your good. (See Romans 8:28.)

You can be in the midst of the biggest storm of your entire life and still feel joy.

Happiness is related to what you have and what you are experiencing. Joy is related to who you know and what He promises to you!

His Confidence

The apostle Paul wrote: *"I am confident of this very thing, that He who began a good work in you will perfect it until the day of Christ Jesus"* (Phil. 1:6).

Our confidence is not based upon our ability or skill or intelligence. Our confidence is based upon the fact that Jesus said He would be with us always and that He would continue to provide for us and protect us and preserve us according to His eternal plan for us. The psalmist said,

> *Though a host encamp against me, my heart will not fear; though war arise against me, in spite of this I shall be confident.* (Ps. 27:3)

In what do you put your confidence?

You are going to be disappointed at some point, at some time...

If you are confident only in yourself and your own limited abilities, skills, knowledge, wisdom, strength, or ability to figure things out.

If you are placing your confidence in another frail, finite, prone-to-error human being.

If you are putting your confidence in an institution or an organization or in a government program.

If you are putting your confidence in the systems of this world, such as the stock market or the ability of negotiators or the legal system.

None of these sources of confidence can guarantee you a sure reward. They can't guarantee that you will get the justice you deserve, the opportunity you desire, or the chance you want to make something of your life. They can't guarantee that you won't fail again.

Your confidence must be in the Lord! He alone can preserve you, protect you, and bring you into great reward. As the Bible says, *"Do not throw away your confidence, which has a great reward"* (Heb. 10:35).

The Battle in Your Mind

Everything I have said to you in this chapter points to this one prevailing truth: Your primary battle against the negative emotional ties that manipulate and control your life is a battle in your mind. God's Word says,

> *For though we walk in the flesh, we do not war according to the flesh, for the weapons of our warfare are not of the flesh, but divinely powerful for the destruction of fortresses. We are destroying speculations and every lofty thing raised up against the knowledge of God, and we are taking every thought captive to the obedience of Christ.* (2 Cor. 10:3–5)

If you perceive that the "battlefield" of your life involves a war with your ex-spouse, you are mistaken. If you think the "war" in your life is one with a person who is in authority over you, you are wrong. Your primary battle against evil is always a battle against the devil, and the battleground is in your mind and heart.

God's Word plainly tells us that the weapons of warfare are not of the flesh, but weapons that are spiritual. With those weapons we are to take down anything that has built itself up as a fortress in our inner spirit. We are to destroy the binding thoughts of "what might have been" or "what might be" or any other thing that takes root in our minds and turns us away from God's truth. We are to take *every thought captive* (2 Cor. 10:5)—to control it completely—and to put it into subjection to the teachings and commandments of Jesus Christ.

There's nothing easy about this battle. It's the toughest battle you will ever face! The good news is that it is a battle God intends for you to win.

God will not tell you to do something you cannot do. People frequently say to me, "I just can't think pure thoughts" or "I can't control my thoughts." Oh, yes, you can!

God does not tell us to do anything that He will not help us do or empower us to do if we will turn to Him and say, "Help me."

As a believer, you have been given the ability—in the Holy Spirit—to put on the garment of praise any time you are feeling depressed or are thinking dark thoughts.

As a believer, you have been given the ability—in the Holy Spirit—to put on an attitude of love any time you are feeling hate.

As a believer, you have been given the ability—in the Holy Spirit—to think positive thoughts any time you are feeling negative about yourself or any other person.

You have the power within you to make a decision to…

Stop playing "our song"—the one you shared with the lover who jilted you.

Stop driving by that person's house.

Stop staring at the old pictures and rereading the old love letters.

You have the power within you to decide that you are going to…

Speak kindly to that person who is trying to undermine your ministry.

Keep your joy even when the boss insists you work late.

Stay positive even when the kids have made a mess and your husband hasn't lifted a finger to help you.

People sometimes wonder why they are sick and don't get well even after great prayers of faith have been prayed over them and they have done everything they know to do medically. In many cases, people remain sick in their bodies because they have refused to let go of damaging negative emotions!

People sometimes wonder why they are always in financial need, even when they pray about their finances and give to God's work. In many cases, people are financially "sick" because they have refused to let go of nagging negativity that leads them to financially unwise behaviors.

People sometimes wonder why they are lonely or why their friends and other loved ones always seem to abandon them. In many cases, people are "sick" in their relationships because they have refused to let go of manipulating emotions that cause them to alienate other people.

Move beyond negativity and choose to release yesterday's pain! Say to your negativity: This party is over; it's time to turn out those lights!

8

Moving beyond Fear

When I was a child, I went to work with my father one day. My dad was a painting contractor and on this particular day, he was working on the exterior of a multistory post office. I went up on the scaffold with him, something I usually enjoyed doing, and then as my father was working—suddenly and without warning—the scaffold began to tip to one side. A tremendous fear gripped me. I was certain we were both about to slide off that scaffold and plummet to the cement below!

My father was able to right that scaffold and secure it. But I was not able to shake the fear I had felt in that moment. It did not leave me even when the incident was over.

That fear, acquired in a very real moment of concern for my safety and well-being, stayed with me. It became a fear associated with all heights. It manifested itself when I got in an elevator—and especially a glass elevator on the exterior of a building. It manifested itself when I boarded an airplane, when I went to eat in a restaurant on an upper floor of a sky-scraper, or even when I went out to stand on a hotel balcony. I felt an overwhelming, powerful fear that I was going to fall to my death. I felt nauseous, weak in my knees, and many times, nearly paralyzed.

My fear of heights became a "spirit" of fear. It hindered my ability to move freely about this world. It kept me from going to certain functions, enjoying certain beautiful views, and taking certain trips with joy and freedom of mobility. Oh, I'd still get on planes and accept hotel accommodations on upper stories of a building. But I didn't have any joy or freedom in my spirit when I found myself in these situations.

That's what a spirit of fear does—it robs you of the joy and freedom that God desires for you to have. It holds you back from receiving the fullness of God's blessings. And it can prevent you from doing what will be a blessing to others.

Some Fears Are Natural—Other Fears Are Not!

There are fears that are natural and helpful. A fear of walking out onto a busy freeway at rush hour is a fear that can be very helpful to the preservation of life. A fear associated with jumping off a three-story roof is a good fear and helpful fear—that fear can save you from serious injury. Natural, normal fears are those that cause you to flee evil, run from danger, and do your best to avoid life-threatening situations.

The fears that shackle us are fears that keep us from making wise decisions or taking godly actions. These fears attempt to take hold of us and control us *in ways that are contrary to the Word of God*. These fears are not helpful. They do nothing to contribute to our experiencing an abundant life in Christ Jesus. Rather, they contribute to our lack of peace, lack of joy, and lack of action. They are fears that become a "spirit of fear" that invades our mind.

Many types of fears can become a "spirit of fear," not just a fear of the evil supernatural realm or the devil and his demons. A fear of financial ruin, a fear of war, a fear associated with family troubles—all types of situations can instill fear in us. The Bible tells us that in the last days,

There will be signs in sun and moon and stars, and upon the earth dismay among nations, in perplexity at the roaring of the sea and the waves, men fainting from fear and the expectation of the things which are coming upon the world; for the powers of the heavens will be shaken. (Luke 21:25–26)

Fear very often throws people into a frenzy; it links with worry and doubt to create great confusion. Just a few years ago, many people in our nation and other parts of the world were caught up in a grip of Y2K fears. We look back now and wonder what all the fuss and bother was about! The fears people had developed as a result of what *might* happen at the turn of the century and millennium—and the dawning of year 2000—turned out to be unfounded. But these fears led many people to begin stockpiling food and water, selling off assets, and upping their dosage of tranquilizers and alcohol and other substances they hoped would help them deal with the dread and stress they felt!

Thousands of people across our nation are caught today in a grip of fear. Some have deep fear about sending their children to school. Others fear losing their jobs or their retirement funds. Others fear war. Others fear an act of terrorism or the spread of a terrible disease in their area.

Take Action Immediately against a Gripping Fear

God's Word tells us that when we feel ourselves sliding into a gripping spirit of fear, we must immediately take a stand against it.

Suppose you have a bad dream in which your wife develops a deadly disease and dies. The moment you awaken from such a nightmare, you may find that your heart is beating rapidly, your breathing is shallow, your hands are clammy. You are scared! What is the first thing you must do? Get on your knees and pray that this thing you dreamed will *not* happen and that you will not live in fear of its happening. Cast down that thing that has taken hold in your subconscious. Speak out in faith against it.

A fear such as this is not rooted in faith; it is rooted in a disbelief that God is able to keep you and your wife in health. Such a fear is contrary to what God's Word says. It tells us that Jesus came to give us an *abundant* life. (See John 10:10.) God's Word says that the Lord preserves life and puts none of the diseases of the enemy on us. (See Exodus 15:26.) You must rise up in your faith and speak out against that thing that comes to grip your mind.

What happens if you allow a fear to develop? You'll continually be looking for the least little symptom of bad health to appear. You'll stay away from crowds so you might not get sick. You may even stop kissing and loving your wife because you fear you might contribute to her ill health. Can you see where such a fear of impending illness might lead if it is allowed to take hold and to grow in a person's mind and heart?

Some people have become so filled with fear of disease they have lived as hermits, totally isolated from society to the best of their ability. They have stopped touching other people or associating with them socially. And where is one's witness of Christ in that? Jesus not only walked freely and confidently among the sick, He reached out and touched those who were considered untouchable—the lepers and the dead! He calls us to do the same—to live boldly and confidently, quick to fellowship with the saints, quick to lay hands on the sick and pray for them, quick to visit people in hospitals, quick to take missions trips to parts of the world that are "unclean."

Suppose you begin to think, "I'm never going to find a good man to marry. I'm always going to be single. I'm never going to have children. I'm going to die a miserable, lonely person." The moment you start to think that way, you need to cry out to God in prayer and cast that fear-instilling thought out of your mind and heart. Speak out in faith against that idea!

Now, it's one thing to be called to be single and celibate for purposes of ministry. There are a few people who are called to live that lifestyle. But for the vast majority of people, a single life is *not* God's plan. God's Word says that the Lord is pleased when a man and woman dwell together in purpose and godly devotion and bear children whom they raise to live lives of purpose and godly devotion! God's Word is all in favor of loving marriages and families. Speak out in your faith against your fear.

Can you see where a fear such as this one might lead? It may very well cause a person to stay at home, refusing to go on that "singles' retreat" or entering into a conversation with a person of the opposite sex. It may cause a person to become extremely withdrawn and isolated. And, in the end, the very fear of being single becomes the reality of having no friends and no social life!

There are people I know who have deep fear that...

• their children will never grow up to adulthood because of the dangers of their neighborhood.

• their son will never get out of jail, and if he does, he won't live a productive, godly life.

• their daughter will never get off drugs.

• their spouse will never turn to the Lord.

The fact is, their fear causes them to relate to their children and spouse in such a way that they help bring about the very state of being they fear.

They tell their children, don't go outside the door, don't engage in your world, don't live your life in boldness. They keep their children from going to church, going to special after-school programs, or going on trips or to camps with church youth. They instill in their children a great mistrust of all people. As a result, their children are scared of their own shadows and have no ability to stand up to a bully or to discern between safe and unsafe situations.

The father who fears his son will never get out of jail says to that boy, "*If* you ever get out of here" instead of "*When* you get out of here." He says to his son, "I don't know what you're going to do. I'm afraid you're going to fall right back into your old ways." This man paints a picture of a difficult world of constant duty and responsibility, rather than painting a picture of a joyous life in Christ in which obedience and responsibility become avenues toward fulfillment, peace, and purpose. He paints a picture of drudgery instead of a picture of positive contribution and meaningful relationships. He is setting his son up to have a negative attitude when he goes before his parole board. He certainly isn't helping his son prepare for the future God has in mind for that young man! He should be saying to that boy, "Here's what you're going to do when you get out of here. Here's the new life I believe God has for you!"

The mother who fears her daughter will never get off drugs treats her daughter as a person who is worthless and hopeless. She doesn't *mean* to do this, but she does it nonetheless. In her attitude and the little things she does when she is with her daughter, she reinforces in her daughter's mind, "I fear you're always going to be in this situation. Woe is me. What did I do to deserve a daughter like you?" What she should be doing is speaking out her faith, "You are sick and God is going to help you get well! You are a blessing to my life, and I'm going to love you and nurture you so you can begin to live out the wonderful talents God has given to you. I'm not going to cover for you, make excuses for you, or participate in lies. I'm going to speak truth to you, pray for you, and do my best to help you discover your full potential in Christ Jesus!"

Rather than live in fear of the current situation, begin to declare with your faith what God says about your future and the future of your loved ones!

Rise up and declare, "God has a purpose and a plan for my child. He is going to bring that to fulfillment!"

Rise up and declare, "My daughter may be pregnant today and not married, but God has something good in store for my daughter in her future. He's going to bring it to pass. Furthermore, you just wait to see what God does through the life of that baby she's carrying!"

Rise up and declare, "My spouse may be out of a job today, but God has a job for him. God is going to help us through this difficult time and provide for us and lead my husband to that job where he can work and receive the rewards and appreciation that are due him!"

Fear Can Create a Self-Fulfilling Prophecy

If you do not rise up in faith, your fear may very well be the beginning point of a self-fulfilling prophecy. People who allow fear to dominate their thoughts will cower in the face of a challenge. They will take no risk, not even a minor one. They will accept no call of God to do something that stretches their faith. They will seek only to "play it safe" in life, never venturing beyond the limits they have already imposed upon themselves. And the end result is failure. The very failure they thought already had them in its grip rises up to grab hold of them in their paralysis.

God's Word tells us, *"For what I fear comes upon me, and what I dread befalls me"* (Job 3:25).

A man named Job is the one who made that statement.

Consider the situation of Job. The Bible tells us that he was a righteous man—the Lord himself described Job as *"a blameless and upright man, fearing God and turning away from evil"* (Job 1:8). Satan said to the Lord, "He's that way because You have blessed him and increased all his possessions. But if You remove Your hand from his life, he'll curse You." The Lord replied, *"Behold, all that he has is in your power; only spare his life"* (Job 2:6). Satan was given permission to destroy what Job owned and possessed, and to destroy Job's health,

133

but Satan was prohibited from taking Job's life. (See Job 1:9–2:6.)

The Bible tells us that Job did not sin nor did he blame God when he lost all that he owned. Job, however, did become discouraged and depressed when his body became covered from head to toe with *"sore boils"* (Job 2:7). I don't know if you've ever had a boil, but people who have had boils tell me that *one* boil will keep them awake at night with pain. To be covered with painful boils would be to live in constant misery.

Job was so miserable he no longer wanted to live. He said, *"Why is light given to him who suffers, and life to the bitter of soul?"* (Job 3:20). He had no desire to eat—in fact, he groaned when food was set before him—and he cried continually. He said, *"I am not at ease, nor am I quiet, and I am not at rest, but turmoil comes"* (v. 26).

In the midst of all these emotions, Job said, *"What I fear comes upon me, and what I dread befalls me"* (v. 25). He had no hope for his future, only dread. He could envision only a future in which the worst would happen to him. A *good* future or a *better* future were not even in his vocabulary at that time, much less a *best* future.

What a picture of a spirit of fear! Unfortunately, it describes many people today.

Four Steps toward Overcoming Fear

Read what the Lord said to Joshua as Joshua prepared to lead the people of God into the land He had promised to give them. Remember as you read that Joshua *knew* this was a land filled with giants because he personally had seen those giants forty years ago. Joshua *knew* that the people had refused to go into the land and that was the reason for their wandering in a wilderness for four decades. Joshua *knew* that battles needed to be fought. The Lord said to Joshua,

Be strong and courageous, for you shall give this people possession of the land which I swore to their fathers to give them. Only be strong and very courageous; be careful to do according to all the law which Moses My servant commanded you; do not turn from it to the right or to the left, so that you may have success wherever you go....Have I not commanded you? Be strong and courageous! Do not tremble or be dismayed, for the LORD your God is with you wherever you go. (Josh. 1:6–7, 9)

What powerful words these are for us today!

In this very brief passage, the Lord tells us precisely *how* we are to move forward in our faith and not give in to fear.

1. Choose *how* you will face fear! The first and foremost thing the Lord said to Joshua was, *"Be strong and courageous!"* He was telling him, in essence, "Take hold of the way you think and feel. Choose how you are going to feel inside. Choose how you are going to think. *Choose* to be strong and courageous."

That's the choice we must make as well. We each must *choose* to confront our fears with our faith.

2. Become certain in your spirit about God's goodness and God's promises to you. The second thing the Lord said was, "Face up to what I have promised to you and believe it, accept it, and receive it." It was one thing for God to say to the children of Israel, "I'm going to give you this land." They could know that in their minds and do nothing about it, and the end result of that would be that they would never enter the land. The children of Israel had to believe that God meant what He said! They had to believe God was going to give them the land. They had to begin to act on that belief.

It is one thing for you to believe God is going to help you get out of debt and pay all your bills on time. You can say, "Yes, I know God wants that for His children." It is something else for you to say, "I know God wants *me* to pay my bills and for *me*

135

to get out of debt." When you know that God wants that blessing for you, you will no longer live in fear of calls from the debt collectors. No, you will begin to seek action to learn how to control your spending and take charge of your debt and begin to do what is necessary to work toward a debt-free life!

It is one thing to believe God wants you as a believer to give your tithe and offerings to His work. You can say, "Yes, I know that's what the Bible says." It is an entirely different matter when you say, "I know God wants *me* to give tithes and offerings. I know God is going to show me how to readjust my priorities in life and curb my spending habits and refigure my budget so I can obey God in this. I know God wants *me* to have the windows of heaven opened up for me and a blessing poured out of my life that will be so great I can't contain it all." (See Malachi 3:10–11.) When you know that God has that financial blessing for you, you are going to start doing what is necessary to move into that blessing.

The same principle holds true for your relationships, your health, your job or career or business, your spiritual life, your ministry, your family. You must accept what God has promised as being true for *you*. You must believe that who God said He is—now and forever—He is for *you*.

Jesus is not just *the* Savior. He must become *your* Savior.

Jesus is not just *the* Lord of all. He must become *your* Lord.

Jesus is not only *the* Source of all blessings. He must become *your* Source of all *"riches in glory"* (Phil. 4:19).

Do you know what God has promised to you today? Are you familiar with the promises in His Word? If you don't know what God has declared to be your rights and privileges as a believer, inform yourself! Get into the Word and read it and study it until you know with certainty what God has promised to you and to every believer.

You must also be 100 percent convinced about the goodness and greatness of God. The Israelites *knew* that God had promised them the land. They *knew* God had helped them and delivered them from their enemies time and time again in the past. They *knew* God had provided manna for their food and water from a rock in taking care of them. They *knew* the very shoe leather of their sandals hadn't worn out. They *knew* God had commanded them to do certain things, to believe certain things, and to have a special relationship with Him. They *knew* God had told them repeatedly that He loved them and wanted only good for them.

But as much as they knew these things, they had to remind themselves often of the truth of what they knew. We must do the same. We must remind ourselves continually of God's goodness and greatness and of His desire to bless us. We must remind ourselves that we are His heirs through Christ Jesus and that He has every good and perfect gift for us in this life, and great eternal rewards waiting for us in the coming life.

How do we remind ourselves of God's promises? By reading aloud the Word of God to our own ears and spirit. By speaking about the goodness and greatness of God. By singing praise songs. By voicing our thanksgiving for all He has done for us, is doing for us, and desires to do in us and through us.

3. Obey God without wavering. The Lord told Joshua not to turn *"to the right or to the left"* (Josh. 1:7) of what He had commanded through the law of Moses. Joshua was told that he should meditate on the book of the law day and night and that it should *"not depart from* [his] *mouth"* (v. 8). In other words, Joshua was to remind himself of God's commandments by speaking them aloud to himself and to others.

Can you recite the Ten Commandments? If not, you need to learn them so you can recite them! Our children recited the Pledge of Allegiance in school every day. How much more

137

important it is for them to recite God's commandments and to quote verses of God's blessing and provision!

What we think about *"day and night"* (Josh. 1:8) and what we speak about *"day and night"* will become the way we live!

If we speak words of absolutely truth, we will walk in that truth.

If we think about what God has directed us to do and the way He has authorized for us to live, we will live that way.

God does not want His children operating according to the latest opinion polls or the latest fads or the latest "politically correct" thinking. God does not want His children operating according to what this person says or that person says. God wants his children living out *His* commandments and *His* principles. He wants us not only to talk the talk of faith but to walk the walk of obedience without wavering or moving to the left or the right. He wants our complete, focused, and committed obedience!

4. Do not tremble or be dismayed. The fourth and final thing the Lord commanded Joshua was that he was not to *"tremble or be dismayed"* (v. 9) because he was to remind himself that God was with him *"wherever* [he would] *go"* (v. 9).

If you lose sight that Jesus is with you always, you will become afraid.

If you lose sight of the fact that the Holy Spirit is in you and that He is greater than anything in the world, you will become fearful. (See 1 John 4:4.)

If you lose sight of the fact that God the Father is *always* available to you to forgive and cleanse you, you will become "dismayed." (See 1 John 1:9.)

It's up to us to remind ourselves that…

- God is with us.
- God is for us.

- God is enabling and empowering us to live godly lives.

- God is the One who takes the release of our faith and causes miracles to flow back toward us.

God never leaves us nor forsakes us, not even for a split second. He is always available to us. He always hears our prayers. He always acts for our eternal good. He is with us wherever we go.

What God commands us to do, He both empowers and enables us to do. God would not have told us to take control over fear and to use our faith to be strong and courageous if we weren't capable of doing so. He would not have given us His promises if He also hadn't given us the ability to receive them, believe them, and act on them. He would not have told us to be unwavering in our obedience if we couldn't be unwavering. He would not have told us to take courage in knowing He was with us if that was an impossible thing to do.

God has told us what to do. He has told us that we are capable of doing it. It's up to us, now, to use our faith and rise up to speak against fear.

Move Forward with Determined Faith!

The moment you begin to move forward with your faith is the moment you begin to be free of the shackles of fear and move into your destiny.

I won't deny that it takes tremendous determination to walk by faith and not by sight. It takes tremendous determination to use your faith, to speak out of your faith, and to act on your faith.

More than a decade ago, God told me that I needed to confront *every* fear I felt in my life and to take authority over it in my faith. I believe He desires that for every believer!

Why?

Your Best Days Are Still Ahead

Because if you do not have the determination in your soul that you are going to life in faith, rather than fear, fear will begin to dominate your mind and heart to the point that you will...

• Make bad decisions to "quickly" get out of negative situations, rather than trusting God for His perfect timing and His wise methods.

• Take the easy way out, which is always a way pleasing to the flesh rather than pleasing to the Holy Spirit.

• Align yourself with people whom you believe to be your security, rather than aligning yourself with God who *is* your security.

• Be reluctant to get out and do what God has called you to do.

When I made a commitment that I was going to face my fears and deal with them in faith, I began to recognize fears in my life that I didn't even know up to that point I had!

I realized that I was afraid to be alone. I had to force myself by faith to take some time and be by myself and choose to like it. The amazing thing I discovered was that God could speak to me much more clearly and powerfully when I was alone with Him than when I was surrounded by people, even godly people!

I realized that I was afraid of riding a roller coaster. I didn't know if that was a fear of falling or not, but I chose to confront that fear. With palms sweating and a lump in my throat the size of a boulder, I went to the amusement park and forced myself to ride the roller coaster over and over until I had no more fear of it.

I realized that I was afraid of riding a motorcycle. Well, you guessed it. I learned how to ride a motorcycle and to overcome that fear to the point where I could feel great joy in getting on that bike and cruising down a mountain highway.

In some ways, I realized I was afraid of opposing the status quo, including what society said about races. I chose to confront that fear with my faith, reaching out to people who were of a different color and culture.

The result?

I enjoy being alone, and I enjoy being with people.

I enjoy having fun on amusement-park rides, I enjoy riding a motorcycle, I enjoy being with people of many different backgrounds, I enjoy my *life,* and I enjoy all that God has created that is for my good!

I have absolutely no doubt that we would not have a multiracial and multicultural church today if I had not faced up to my fears and cast them down with my faith.

I was determined and remain determined that *no* fear will control me. Only God will control me. I will do what He tells me to do, go wherever He tells me to go, give up or take on or lay aside or pick up whatever He directs me to do.

I will *not* have negative, debilitating, manipulating fears ruling my life. I will *not* have any fears yanking me about. I choose to move beyond yesterday's pain. I live in faith, knowing that my best days are still ahead!

What about you?

9

Moving beyond Bitterness

In recent years, literally hundreds of articles have been written about the link between bitterness and other negative emotions and poor health—not only poor spiritual and emotional health, but poor physical health. The phrase "root of bitterness" has been used to describe the origin of numerous ailments that infect relationships and organizations.

One question, however, is rarely addressed: What causes bitterness? I meet many people who know bitterness when they see or hear it in others. I meet people who tell me that they know how bitterness feels because they have felt it or are feeling it. And there are countless others who don't recognize bitterness in themselves because they don't know the origins of bitterness.

Bitterness arises when someone believes that life has treated him unjustly or unfairly. It begins to take hold of a person at the time he experiences a hard time, a difficulty, or a tragedy. It develops when there's unjustness or unfair dealings in the aftermath of that hard time.

The fact is, all of us have a potential for developing bitterness because we all face hard times and unjust or unfair situations at some point in our lives.

No person is immune from trouble, not even the most successful or seemingly "secure" person.

Look at Daniel, for instance, who was a major political figure in Babylon. Even so, he was thrown into a lions' den. (See Daniel 6.)

Consider Daniel's friends—Shadrach, Meshach, and Abed-Nego—who also were key political leaders in Babylon. They, like Daniel, were known for their godly behavior and faith. Even so, they were thrown into a burning, fiery furnace. (See Daniel 3.)

And then there was King David, who knew great success not only on the battlefield, but also as a king. He was known for His desire to do what was right before the Lord and for his faith. Even so, he still had to flee for his life when his son Absalom led a rebellion against him. (See 2 Samuel 15.)

The automatic response when situations such as these occur is to feel discouragement. And there's nothing wrong with that immediate emotional response. Discouragement is an emotion that is intended by God to be a signal to us that we need to start praising and thanking God so that our confidence and faith will rise up within us.

What happens, however, is that most people who feel discouragement do not turn to God and trust Him *more*. Rather, they stop trusting God and starting blaming Him, or they turn away from God and to other people. Often, they will stop taking responsibility for their own lives and start blaming others.

Are You Blaming or Trusting God?

One of the major lies of the devil is that God cannot be trusted. It's the first trick he pulled in the Garden of Eden. The first statement that the devil made to Eve is also the first question in the Bible: *"Has God said?"* (Gen. 3:1). The implication of the Bible was that God couldn't be trusted to be true to His word.

Never lose sight of the reality that the devil is a liar. Jesus said about the devil, *"He was a murderer from the beginning, and does not stand in the truth, because there is no truth in him. Whenever he speaks a lie, he speaks from his own nature; for he is a liar, and the father of lies"* (John 8:44).

The devil's lies to us and about us are persistent and unrelenting. They always strike at the point where we are most vulnerable or weak. Many of the lies of the devil are related to our success—they are ones that point to and magnify our past failures. The devil tells us…

• You aren't worthy of God's forgiveness. You can't trust God to forgive you as He has said He would.

• You don't deserve God's love. You can't trust God to love you—not all the time, regardless of what you do.

• You can never become a success. You can't trust God to make a way for you to use your talents and feel fulfillment in your life.

• You have such terrible built-in flaws that you will never be able to overcome them. You cannot be changed or healed. God made you that way—He has always known you'd never amount to anything. You can't trust God to make you whole.

• You will never fulfill God's destiny for you. You can't trust God to lead you and guide you into the realization of your potential.

The devil is a liar.

The truth is, God is always trustworthy.

The truth is, you *can* choose to trust God.

The truth is, anything the devil tells you that you can't do, can't have, or won't ever become is usually the opposite of what is true! The very things he tells you that you can't do are the things you likely *can* do. The things the devil says you can't have are very likely the things God wants you to have!

145

Your Best Days Are Still Ahead

The very things he tells you that you won't become may be the things God has planned for you from the beginning.

Now...

You might lose your car.

You might lose your house.

You might lose your spouse.

You might lose a loved one to death.

But there's one thing that nobody and no circumstance can take from you and that's your ability to *choose* to trust God.

God Always Deals First with the Trust Issue

Most of us want God to rush right in and "fix" whatever is wrong with us—we want Him to heal us, shower prosperity upon us, give us the relationships we want, and so forth. God, however, always starts first with the trust issue. He will go to great lengths to bring us to the point where we are willing to trust Him with everything—very often before He gives us *anything* we seek.

Over and over, when the Israelites failed to trust God, God provided a way for them to have their basic needs met, but He also allowed them to face circumstances, such as slavery and war, that would bring them back to Him.

When the Israelites failed to trust God to give them a victory in Canaan, the land God had promised to give them, God provided a way for them to have their basic needs met, but He also allowed them to wander for forty years in the wilderness.

Time and again, as recorded in the book of Judges, when the Israelites failed to put God first and turned to other gods, He allowed them to be subjected to the very harsh oppression of foreign enemies. But He provided a way of escape for them.

Every time they repented and returned to worship the Lord, God sent a judge to bring about their deliverance. And as long as the people sought to keep His commandments, they prospered in the land God had given them.

Don't despair if you are going through a very hard time. Face up to three tough questions.

1. What Caused the Hard Time? In many cases, if you are really honest with yourself, you may very well be experiencing difficulty as a result of your own rebellion, sin, or failure to put God first. You may be reaping the consequences of failing to believe that God desires your success, failing to obey God, or failing to walk in faith before God. If that's the case, confess your rebellion or sin to God, and ask Him to forgive you. If you have been failing to believe God desires your success, confess your fault and ask God to help you to believe. If you have failed to keep God's commandments, even though you knew better, confess your disobedience to God. Change your ways. Begin to keep His commandments. If you have failed to walk in faith, start walking! Start trusting God to lead and guide you. Trust Him to help you live out the life of blessing He has for you. Don't give up in your faith walk!

2. How Might God Use this Hard Time? Recognize that God can and is using this hard time to teach you, purify you, and prepare you for what He has ahead for you. The key difference between punishment and chastisement is this: In punishment, the person who is being punished experiences pain or loss because the person doing the punishing is exerting authority in order to bring about a specific outcome. As an example, a dictator might kill a particular group of people in order to show that he will not tolerate any rebellion against his rule.

Chastisement is very different. The person who is being chastised may experience some pain or loss but the reason for that is to teach a lesson intended for the ultimate improvement, education, refinement, or betterment of the person.

The one doing the chastising has the good of the person being chastised in mind.

God chastises His children because He loves them. If you are going through a difficult period, God has allowed you to experience it for a purpose—and the purpose is for your *good*. Ask the Lord what He is trying to teach you or show you.

I recently met someone who told me he thought it was just fine for a Christian to smoke marijuana. That could be the reason that person is in a wilderness.

I know a woman who believes it is perfectly acceptable for a Christian to date non-Christians. That could be the reason she feels she is in a wilderness.

God has a way of getting our attention in order to change some of our beliefs!

Some people need to clean up their lives physically—getting rid of things that pollute and cause damage to the body—before God will allow them to experience greater health.

Some people need to get over a former relationship and be healed of all the emotional hurt they have experienced before God will send someone new into their lives.

It's not enough to ask God to show you what it is that He is desiring to do in you during a difficult time. You must also agree to make the changes He requires you to make!

3. What Change Needs to Be Made? As the Lord reveals what it is that He desires for you to learn or change in your life, be quick to make that change. Don't try to justify your past behavior. Don't make excuses for yourself. Own up to what it is that God says you need to change and start making those changes! Be quick to repent.

The sooner you yield to what it is that God desires to do in your life, the sooner the difficult period will be over and you can move forward into the greater blessing He has for you.

Some people need to learn how to handle money before God will trust them with more money.

Some people need to learn how to deal with their explosive anger before God will trust them with the blessing of having children of their own.

Look for God to talk to you about the direction your life is going, the people you are keeping company with, the depth of your faith, the way you are living your life. Ask Him to speak to you as you read your Bible, go to church to hear godly preaching, or listen to Bible-based, Spirit-anointed teachings on television, radio, or cassette tape. Open your spiritual ears to hear what God has to say to you.

Oh, you may not like it. In fact, I can pretty much guarantee that you *won't* like some of what you hear. But own up to the fact that God speaks only truth to you.

God will never lie to you and tell you that some sins are acceptable in His sight. He will never lie to you and tell you that you can sin without reaping negative consequences.

God will never lie to you and tell you that you are a hopeless case. He will never lie to you and say that you can live any old way you choose and still be blessed.

No, God will speak the truth to you about who you are, where you are in your faith walk, how He desires for you to change, and with whom He wants you to associate. He will make very clear the path of clean living, honest work, godly relationships, joyful worship, and edifying teaching. If you are sincere in asking, "Lord, what do You want me to change in my life?"—He'll tell you!

Some people have asked me, "How can I tell if it is really God speaking to me?" His directions to you will always be in full agreement with the Word of God. God does not say one thing in the Bible and then whisper something other than that to your heart. His desire for you is always that you live in full agreement with His commandments, principles, and promises.

When God shows you what it is that He wants you to learn or change, go to His Word for confirmation. Don't go to your friend who will tell you anything he knows you want to hear. Don't go to your relatives who love you and won't say anything that they think might hurt you. Go to the Word. See what the Word has to say about what you heard God speak to your spirit.

As you seek God for direction, be sure to...

Ask God "When?"

Don't try to push God's timetable. God has a set time and a sequence of events that are necessary for you to follow if you are to reach the level of success He desires for you to experience.

You may need some training or some more information before God can move you into that job He wants you to have.

You may need to move out of the neighborhood in which you have been living before God can put you into association with the person He wants you to meet and marry.

You may need to get into a Bible-believing, Spirit-anointed church before God can teach you the lessons He wants you to learn so He can open up the opportunity He has for you.

A man said to me not long ago, "I never thought much about where God might want me to work. I just took the first job I could get." There are times when that is what a person needs to do—that job may very well be God's immediate answer of provision. But in this man's case I knew it was God speaking through me when I said, "It's obvious that you are unhappy, unfulfilled, unrewarded, and unappreciated in the job you have. I suggest you start asking God where He wants you to work *next.*"

Ask God to lead you step-by-step. Don't expect to become an overnight wonder. Those who experience "overnight success" are very often those who later experience "overnight failure."

If you are facing a major decision, such as marriage or where to go to college or what to undertake as a career....

If you are desiring to make a major purchase, such as a house or car or a business...

If you are facing a major change of any type in your life, such as retirement or a major change in your job or going back to school or getting a job after many years of raising your children...

Ask God, "Is this Your timing?"

Ask God, "Am I putting things in the right sequence?"

Ask God, "Is there a specific plan You want me to follow that will take me through a series of steps to get where You want me to end up?"

Ask God "How?"

God not only has a timetable for you to move out of failure into the full success He has for you, but He also has a preferred *method* for you to use.

Some people need to go to college to get the education they need for the work God wants them to do. Other people need to go to a vocational-technical school, get a job as an apprentice, or go to a Bible college or church-related training institute.

Some people need a teacher or a mentor to help them develop specific skills. Other people need to look for places to practice their craft or display their talents and "learn by doing."

Some people need to save up for a major purchase and pay cash. Others need to get a loan they can repay over time.

Ask God, "*How* do you want me to go about making the changes you are leading me to make? *How* do you want me to grow?"

Ask God "Whom?"

God never does things for just one person alone. Your life is connected to the lives of other people no matter what you are doing. God isn't going to bless you without desiring that you become a blessing to others around you. God isn't going to ask you to move a mountain without handing out some shovels to other people to help you move that mountain.

Ask God, "Whom do You want me to work for or with? Whom do You want me to help, bless, teach, or minister to? Whom do You want me to learn from?"

Whom does God want to be your customers, clients, patients, students, associates, employees, employers? Whom does God want to be your spouse, your friends?

A woman said to me not long ago, "It never dawned on me to ask God if the man I married was the man *He* wanted me to marry." I said, "That could be at the heart of the problems you are having today."

Stop Blaming and Complaining

One thing that you absolutely must do to live free of bitterness is to quit playing the "blame and complain" game.

Time and again we read that the Israelites "murmured" against God. At times the word is translated as "quarreled" or "grumbled." (See Exodus 17:3 as an example.) We would probably use the word *complained*. You can also substitute words and phrases such as *strident criticism, derision, grumbling,* or *griping.*

Murmuring comes from an argumentative, negative, disgruntled spirit.

If you want to stay out of bitterness, don't murmur or complain about your situation. The problem with murmuring is that God takes it personally even if you aren't specifically mentioning Him in your murmuring! When the Israelites were wandering in the wilderness, they seemed to go from one bout of murmuring to the next. They always seemed to be finding something to complain about or blame God for. There isn't a single mention of their murmuring to which God responded, "Oh well, isn't that cute?" To the contrary, God always put them in a difficult bind so that they stopped their murmuring!

Don't pout when things don't go your way.

Don't throw yourself a pity party when you find yourself in a difficult position.

Don't throw up your hands and say, "Why me?" and then sit down and wallow in your tears when you find yourself experiencing a hard time.

And don't get into the blame game. Don't blame God for the mess you are in. Don't blame others for the trouble you are having. Don't point your finger at anyone other than the person staring back at you in the mirror.

Accept your responsibility for your failure.

But then, don't gripe and grumble about it. Don't keep talking about it. Get up, square your shoulders, put a smile on your face, go to God about it, get His wisdom on the positive direction you are to take, and then get busy doing what He shows you to do!

I recently heard about a man who is still complaining bitterly about a financial setback he had fourteen years ago. He's still blaming a former employer for firing him and causing him to lose his job and his seniority and have to start over. The fact is, this man has done more complaining than working in the last fourteen years. He is still putting out

153

energy talking about and blaming his former employer when he *should* be extending himself for his current employer!

I know people who are still murmuring about how terrible their lives are in the aftermath of a divorce. They can't seem to quit grumbling about all they have lost and how unfairly they were treated. The fact is, they are doing more complaining than they are seeking to be healed of their emotional pain. They are wasting more energy talking about past relationships than investing themselves in building new ones!

Put in a New Tape

Stop talking about the things that someone did to you in the past that caused you to feel hurt, rejection, hatred, or anger. The more you bring up what happened to you in the past, the more you reopen the wounds in your heart.

There comes a point where you must let go of what happened to you. Stop talking about it to every person you meet. Stop bringing it up in conversations with the person who hurt you. Stop referring to it. Stop using it as an excuse. Stop using it as a reason for justifying your failures.

Yes, you may have been abused.

Yes, you may have been abandoned.

Yes, you may have been rejected.

Yes, you may have been treated in a manner that was unjust, unfair, or very hurtful.

But now what?

You can't change what has happened to you. But you *can* determine where you are going. Focus on what God has ahead for you rather than what others have done to you in your past.

As long as you continue to talk about what happened to you as a child or in a bad relationship or in a former situation, you are going to remain locked into bitterness. You will be setting the stage to relive all the old harmful feelings.

Change the topic! Put in a new tape! Don't keep going back over and over and over and over what caused you to feel bitter in the first place.

Guard What You Say

The vast majority of people don't give any forethought to what they say. They just open their mouths and blurt out whatever comes to mind. You must guard the words of your mouth if you are going to live free of bitterness.

God's Word says,

Death and life are in the power of the tongue.
(Prov. 18:21)

Not what enters into the mouth defiles the man, but what proceeds out of the mouth, this defiles the man.
(Matt. 15:11)

The tongue is a fire, the very world of iniquity; the tongue is set among our members as that which defiles the entire body, and sets on fire the course of our life, and is set on fire by hell.
(James 3:6)

Your words are judged by God just as much as your deeds.

Your words determine your success just as much as your work.

Your words reflect your character just as much as your behavior.

Even if you don't understand what's happening to you…

Even if you don't fully understand God's purposes for allowing you to go through a failure or a hard time…

Your Best Days Are Still Ahead

Even if you feel lower than you've ever felt...

Make up your mind to speak out of your *faith* and not your failure. Begin to say,

• "God is going to turn things around for me and my family."

• "God is going to show me what to do."

• "God is going to reverse this curse."

• "God is going to make a way where there doesn't seem to be a way."

• "I'm not always going to be poor or in debt."

• "I'm not always going to feel discouraged."

• "I'm not always going to be uneducated or unskilled."

• "I'm not always going to live on welfare."

• "I'm not always going to be in poor health."

• "I will never give up. I'm not going to back up."

Get Your Eyes Back on God's Greater Goals

At the beginning of this chapter I reminded you that Daniel; Shadrach, Meshach, and Abed-Nego; and King David each knew hard times even when they were at the height of their personal success. Let me also remind you that each of these men remained faithful to God. They trusted God in their time of great tribulation. And God acted on their behalf.

Daniel came out of that lions' den unmarked, and he was entrusted by God with tremendous visions about the future. Shadrach, Meshach, and Abed-Nego came out of that fiery furnace "unsinged" and without even the smell of smoke on them, and they were given even greater authority. David regained his throne in Jerusalem, and he lived to see his son Solomon succeed him on the throne.

Never doubt that God is fully capable of bringing you all the way through the wilderness to a time of joy and prosperity.

God did not leave the Israelites in Egypt. He didn't leave them in the wilderness. For that matter, He didn't leave them in Babylon when they were carried off by the Babylonians. Throughout the Bible, we find example after example of times when the Israelites turned from God, experienced great tribulation, returned to God in repentance, and then were restored by God to a position of blessing.

God has a goal for you that is greater than today's trouble.

Continue to walk in freedom, with no strings of bitterness attached. Continue to pursue God's greater goals. Continue to believe for God's best. Your best days *are* still ahead!

10

Moving beyond Depression

No matter who you are, you have experienced, are experiencing, or will experience times in your life when you face the blues—disappointments, sadness, and even depression. Any time life doesn't turn out the way we think it should or the way we have planned, we can feel discouraged.

Any time we don't reach our dreams, we can feel disappointed.

Any time we feel that life is unfair, we can feel devastated.

Any time we do everything we know to do and in spite of our best efforts, things don't happen the way we had hoped they would happen, we can feel discouraged.

Many times I have felt absolutely certain that God was going to do something, and it didn't happen the way I had thought. Many times I have prayed and trusted God, and then have been disappointed at the immediate results. And I readily admit, in those times I have felt the blues.

The breakup of a relationship…

The loss of a loved one…

A divorce…

Financial setbacks…

Being single with no prospects in sight…

Being married to a person who is abusive…

Each of these situations and countless others can result in a person's feeling down and asking: "Why me? What's life all about? What's the use in trying?"

If discouragement stays long enough, it can steal your dreams, dash your hopes, quench your joy, turn you away from your purpose for living, and ultimately rob you of your destiny.

Don't Deny Your Depression

One of the worst things you can do is deny that you are feeling down. I've met people who insist, "I'm a Christian and Christians don't get depressed." The fact is, Christians can and do get depressed! In denying your depression, you are just stalling your recovery from it.

Nobody is ever so spiritually mature that he or she is immune from depression.

For example, Elijah had done a great work for God. He had confronted all the false prophets, psychics, and astrologers of the land in a showdown on the top of Mount Carmel. He had revealed that the priests who had led the people astray in worship to the false god Baal had no real power, and, in the end, Elijah had killed all these so-called "prophets of Baal" single-handedly.

In the aftermath of this experience, Elijah was exhausted. When he heard the threats of Queen Jezebel against his life for what he had done, he felt fear.

In exhaustion and fear, Elijah ran away—he literally ran for his life all the way to Beersheba, more than a hundred miles away, and there, he said to the Lord, *"Take my life"* (1 Kings 19:4). Elijah had reached the end of his rope. He felt he couldn't take any more. In his exhaustion, fear, and depression, Elijah sat down under a juniper tree and said to the Lord what many people today are saying, "I've had enough. I just can't take one more thing. God please let me die. I'd be better off dead." (See 1 Kings 18:37–19:4.)

Even Christians can reach the place in their downward spiral of exhaustion, fear, and discouragement that they say—perhaps only inwardly—"I've had enough. I'd just as soon go on and be with the Lord."

Elijah was so depressed that he hid in a cave.

That's exactly what the enemy would have you do! He wants you to become so depressed that you will isolate yourself, pull the shades down over the windows of your house, quit answering the telephone, and there, in the darkness of your own home and the darkness of your own soul, wallow in misery and self-pity. If he can get you to do that, he will have rendered you ineffective in your witness for Christ Jesus. He will have put a stop to your songs of praise, your prayers of thanksgiving, your inner joy, your influence, your work, your ministry, your outreach, your sharing of the Gospel. He will have put a stop to those aspects of your life that are the most positive and eternal.

Explore the Root Causes

Depression is a symptom of something that is wrong in your life. It is not the real problem. It is only the signal that there's a problem deep inside you that you need to deal with. If you are feeling blue today, recognize that your depression is the offspring or the fruit of a problem. Set yourself to discovering what the root of your depression is, and then deal with that root.

Take time to examine your life. Don't expect others to pray a "magic" prayer over your life to free you from depression. Seek first the healing or forgiveness of the root cause of your depression. The underlying root that produces the fruit of depression may lie in the physical, emotional, or spiritual realm. To truly address depression, you need to know its origin.

Physical Causes of Depression

A physical problem, such as lack of sleep, poor diet, sickness, or a chemical imbalance, can cause depression. If you allow yourself to routinely become too tired or malnourished as the result of eating or drinking the wrong kinds of foods and beverages, you can feel depressed.

People who are routinely sick tend to become depressed. Get to the root cause of your sickness. If your sickness is caused by bad habits of eating, change those habits. If it is caused by the use of alcohol or drugs or the overuse of prescription medication, get help for your addiction. Ask the Lord to show you what you must do to be free of all forms of chemical dependency.

People who routinely overwork themselves into exhaustion become depressed. Ask yourself, "Why am I overworking?" Are you trying to meet some deep inner need to feel worthy or valuable? Are you trying to win the approval of others, including God, by overachieving? Have you been incorrectly taught that you should never relax or enjoy times of recreation because to have fun is a sin? Get to the root reason for your exhaustion. If it's simply a matter of bad scheduling or an undisciplined life, get your life in order. Start using your time well. If your weariness has an emotional need at its root, ask the Lord to show you how you might have those needs met by Him so you won't need to strive and struggle to the point of exhaustion.

People who have very bad eating habits—often evidenced by consuming too much sugar—are people who can easily fall into a pattern of sugar-related highs and lows. A "sugar low" can feel virtually the same as depression. If you suspect this problem in your life, take action. Learn how to eat in such a way that your blood sugar is evened out and you have adequate energy all day. Ask the Lord to show you where to go to get the information you need and to help you to discipline yourself in what you eat and drink.

Emotional Causes of Depression

An emotional or relational problem can be the origin of depression. If you are stifling feelings of anger, loneliness, or hatred, you can easily fall into depression.

A persistent grudge or constant feelings of bitterness will always bring a person down. Unforgiveness is also a root cause of depression. So is fear.

We move from discouragement to depression when we begin to fear that things aren't going to work out as we had hoped.

We move from discouragement to depression when we begin to fear that God isn't going to respond the way we wanted Him to respond.

We move from discouragement to depression when we begin to fear that God isn't going to hear us or answer our prayers.

We move from discouragement to depression when we begin to fear that we are going to lose more than we are going to gain or regain; that we are going to sink, not swim; that we are on a downward slope of deprivation, loss, or destruction that cannot be reversed in spite of our great desire otherwise.

Always recognize that faith is the opposite of fear, and ultimately, faith is the cure for depression that is rooted in emotional problems such as fear. Forgiveness is the cure for depression that is rooted in emotional problems associated with hate, anger, and bitterness.

163

Spiritual Causes of Depression

Sin can be a likely cause of depression. When you are engaged in any form of behavior that grieves or brings sorrow to the Holy Spirit, you are very prone to feeling the blues. The Holy Spirit's convicting power often produces a heaviness of spirit or a feeling of restless frustration deep within that can be interpreted by a person as discouragement or sadness.

Don't misinterpret what God is trying to do in you. He isn't putting depression on you. He's trying to get you to deal with someone who needs to be confronted, forgiven, or possibly removed from your life or some issue that needs to be addressed so that you can move into the greater blessings He has ahead for you.

What is it that grieves the Holy Spirit? The apostle Paul wrote this to the church in Ephesus:

Let no unwholesome word proceed from your mouth, but only such a word as is good for edification according to the need of the moment, that it may give grace to those who hear. And do not grieve the Holy Spirit of God, by whom you were sealed for the day of redemption. Let all bitterness and wrath and anger and clamor and slander be put away from you, along with all malice. And be kind to one another, tender-hearted, forgiving each other, just as God in Christ also has forgiven you. (Eph. 4:29–32)

If unwholesome words are coming out of your mouth, they are an indication that you are feeling anger, bitterness, resentment, hatred, or revenge deep inside your heart. God's Word tells us, *"Watch over your heart with all diligence, for from it flow the springs of life"* (Prov. 4:23). Jesus said,

There is no good tree which produces bad fruit; nor, on the other hand, a bad tree which produces good fruit. For each tree is known by its own fruit....The good man out

164

of the good treasure of his heart brings forth what is good; and the evil man out of the evil treasure brings forth what is evil; for his mouth speaks from that which fills his heart.
(Luke 6:43–45)

If your heart is filled with negative emotions, you are going to find your speech polluted and your behavior poisonous to others around you. That is not godly behavior, and the Holy Spirit will move immediately to convict you to alter your attitude, deal with your negative feelings, clean up your language, and change your behavior!

What did the apostle Paul mean by unwholesome words? He meant the speaking of anything that doesn't help you or another person become more whole in body, mind, spirit, and relationships. Things that are wholesome build up, strengthen, and produce wholeness in us and in others.

Unwholesome words include gossip, murmuring against those in authority, using swear words and filthy language of all kinds, slander and lies against a person's character or motives, and any other kind of negative language that tears down a person's faith, hope, or ability to feel and express love.

Unwholesome words include outbursts of anger that leave the listener feeling devastated and wounded, even if no physical blows were struck.

Unwholesome words include words of harsh judgment and criticism that can deeply wound another person's heart and cause him to lose heart.

Any word that is not spoken with kindness, with an attitude of tenderhearted love, and in a spirit of forgiveness is an unwholesome word!

When we speak in an unwholesome way, we grieve the Holy Spirit, and He will move immediately to convict us. The more we resist Him—refuse to seek God's forgiveness, refuse

165

to acknowledge our need to make changes—the stronger the convicting power will become. God's purpose is not to drag us down, but to bring us to the point where we will humble ourselves before Him, repent of our ways, and move forward with godly behavior, which Paul identified as being *"kind to one another, tender-hearted, forgiving each other"* (Eph. 4:32).

Check your "sin thermometer." If you are routinely engaged in sin and are feeling the heavy convicting power of the Holy Spirit, you may very well feel depressed.

Trust Issues and Depression

In the vast majority of cases, depression is a signal that there's a breakdown of some type in a person's relationship with the Lord. Those who are strong in their relationship to God are strong in faith. And those who are strong in faith are not defeated by fear or doubt.

The question you need to ask in your relationship is not, "Where did God go?" but, "What have I done to cause a breakdown in my relationship with the Lord?"

God's Word says, *"The LORD will not abandon His people"* (1 Sam. 12:22).

The promise of God is, *"I WILL NEVER DESERT YOU, NOR WILL I EVER FAIL YOU OR FORSAKE YOU"* (Heb. 13:5). (See also Deuteronomy 31:6.)

Jesus said, *"I am with you always"* (Matt. 28:20).

He also said, *"I will not leave you as orphans; I will come to you"* (John 14:18).

And Jesus said about the Holy Spirit, *"I will ask the Father, and He will give you another Helper, that He may be with you forever"* (v. 16).

No, God doesn't leave us. He doesn't abandon the relationship.

166

We are the ones who do the leaving, the withdrawing, the moving away.

Many people like to blame situations or circumstances for the distance they feel in their relationship with the Lord. The truth is, no situation or circumstance has the power to drive a wedge between you and the Lord. No demon or human enemy can cause a breakdown in your relationship with the Lord.

Let me remind you of this powerful passage in God's Word:

> *Who shall separate us from the love of Christ? Shall tribulation, or distress, or persecution, or famine, or nakedness, or peril, or sword? Just as it is written, "For Thy sake we are being put to death all day long; we were considered as sheep to be slaughtered." But in all these things we overwhelmingly conquer through Him who loved us. For I am convinced that neither death, nor life, nor angels, nor principalities, nor things present, nor things to come, nor powers, nor height, nor depth, nor any other created thing, shall be able to separate us from the love of God, which is in Christ Jesus our Lord.* (Rom. 8:35–39)

Nothing has the power to separate us from God's love. Except what we do or don't do. Our fear, our doubt, our neglect of our prayer life, our failure to read God's Word— these things that are totally within our control are the only things that can push God away.

Invite God back into your life—into every area of your life and into every area of your thinking and believing!

Stop trying to go it alone. Instead,

> *Trust in the Lord with all your heart, and do not lean on your own understanding. In all your ways acknowledge Him, and He will make your paths straight.* (Prov. 3:5–6)

Regain an Awareness of Your God-Given Potential

Years ago, a mother shared with me a story about her daughter, who had been a sophomore in college when this incident took place. The daughter, Regina, had come home for a month-long break between semesters sorely depressed. She took to her bed and stayed there—sometimes sleeping eighteen hours a day. When she wasn't in bed, she moped about the house in her pajamas and robe. She had no ambition to get dressed and leave the house. She had no desire to see friends.

"One day I just had enough of it," said Regina's mother. "I marched right into her room, opened the curtains, threw back the covers of her bed and said, 'Get up!'"

"What did she do?" I asked.

"She got up!" her mother laughed. "She thought something must be terribly wrong for me to talk to her that way."

Her mother continued, "Before she could get back into that bed, I was pulling off the covers. I said, 'I'm washing these sheets and while I'm washing them, I want you to get yourself dressed. Put on some makeup and fix your hair. We're going somewhere.'"

"What did she do?" I asked.

"She got herself ready. I think she thought I was taking her to a doctor, and she wouldn't have minded that. Instead, I went down to the homeless shelter. When we got there, I said, 'Get out of the car.' And when she got out, I locked the door behind. I rolled down the window just a couple of inches and I said, 'I'll be back for you in three hours.' Regina looked at me as if I had lost my mind, and then she got angry. 'What are you talking about?' she said. 'Do you mean to tell me you are abandoning me here?'

"I said, 'No, girl, I'm not abandoning you. They are expecting you inside there. I'm just dropping you off.'

"Regina said back to me, 'They are expecting me to be a homeless person for three hours? What are you trying to do to me?'

"I said, "No, they aren't expecting you to *be* a homeless person. They are expecting you to *help* the homeless people. I told them what a smart, talented young woman you are. I told them you had a lot to offer other people. They were excited to hear that and they said they could use your help. So I'm dropping you off so you can help the homeless people inside that building. I'll be back for you in three hours."

"What happened?" I asked. I could see Regina standing there on the sidewalk, angry and upset. I knew this girl, and she had something of an attitude and a temper at that time. I could just imagine what she was saying and doing.

"Well," her mother said, "I came back in three hours, and I had my old Regina back. She wasn't waiting for me on the sidewalk where I had left her. I had to go into the building and find her. She was working with some children of a homeless woman, and I practically had to drag her away from them. They kept asking her, 'When are you coming back?' and she finally looked at me and said, 'So, when am I coming back?' I said, 'When do you want to come back?' She said, 'Tomorrow.'

"And that's the way it was, Bishop. I took her there for the next fifteen days, including Sunday afternoons. If you ask me, the cure for depression is to get busy helping somebody else. It's getting your eyes back on all the talents and abilities God has given you, and then using those talents and abilities to make things better for someone else."

I couldn't agree more.

God has a purpose for your life.

I don't care what anybody may have told you in the past; hear this truth deep in your spirit today: God has a purpose for *your* life.

Your Best Days Are Still Ahead

I don't care if you were a crack baby, an illegitimate child, a former drug user, a former prostitute, a high school drop-out, a convicted criminal, or a victim of any other negative situation that people may have held up to you as a reason you can't succeed.

God has made you in such a way that you are unique and you are equipped to reach people with a message of His love, delivering power, and forgiveness that nobody else is as well-equipped to reach.

Make no doubt about it. You have a spiritual enemy and part of his work against you is to convince you that nobody will ever love you again, nobody will ever hire you again, nobody will ever take you seriously again, nobody will ever help you again.

God's truth is that you *will* love again, you *will* work again, you *will* experience purpose and joy again *if* you are willing to give some of what you have to those who have even less than you have. If you are willing to give some of who you are to others who need a friend, a mentor, an advisor, or a helper, you will find that you are less and less depressed.

Get Your Eyes Back on Jesus

Another vital thing you must do is regain your focus on Jesus Christ, your Savior and your Lord.

Depression causes a person to turn inward rather than upward to God, looking ahead to a brighter future or outward to helping another person. Depression is very self-focused. It causes a person to spend all his or her time and energy on answering the question, "How can I get *my* needs met?"

The question that pulls a person out of depression is, "What does Jesus want to do in me?"

Your spiritual enemy wants you to get your eyes off Jesus and onto your circumstances. Your spiritual enemy will do everything in his power to undermine your relationship with Jesus. He will do all he can to bind you to the fact that Jesus alone is your...

- Savior

- Deliverer

- Healer

- Restorer

- Provider

- Protector

- Strength

King David, who knew what it meant to be delivered from his enemies time and time again, sang a great praise song to the Lord in which he said,

> The LORD is my rock and my fortress and my deliverer; my God, my rock, in whom I take refuge; my shield and the horn of my salvation, my stronghold and my refuge; my savior.   (2 Sam. 22:2–4)

Note that David used one little word ten times in these four short verses: *"my."* David had a *relationship* with God. He trusted Him to provide everything he needed, when he needed it, and in the form that was to David's best advantage!

God's Word says,

> Do you not know? Have you not heard? The Everlasting God, the LORD, the Creator of the ends of the earth does not become weary or tired. His understanding is inscrutable. He gives strength to the weary, and to him who lacks might He increases power.   (Isa. 40:28–29)

What you don't have, God has for you.

Are you physically exhausted? He has renewal and refreshment for you.

Are you confused? He has understanding and answers for you.

Are you weary from carrying a heavy emotional load? He has strength and restoration for you.

Are you struggling to reach up just so you can touch bottom? God has an increase for you.

How do we put ourselves into position to receive all that God has for us?

We wait on Him. We spend time in His presence. We spend time in His Word. We spend time in prayer. We trust Him as we wait for Him to act on our behalf.

Isaiah 40:31 is a verse worth your memorizing and speaking often:

Those who wait for the LORD will gain new strength; they will mount up with wings like eagles, they will run and not get tired, they will walk and not become weary.

God has no desire for you to continue to sit in the dark cave of your depression. God takes no delight in the fear and doubt that have you defeated. Your depression brings Him no glory. No!

God's desire is for you to get strong, to soar, to succeed, to endure!

Activate Your Faith

When you regain an awareness of your God-given potential and you get your eyes back on Jesus, you will have taken two giant steps toward activating your faith. When you truly see that God has a plan and purpose for your life—He has work for you to do and things for you to accomplish—and when you truly are in close relationship with Him so that you know He is with you every step of the way as you fulfill your destiny, you *can't* stay down!

Faith and depression cannot coexist in the same heart.

Faith is not an emotion. It is a decision of the will. You have to *decide* that you are going to believe God's promise, trust in God to bring those promises to fulfillment in your life, begin to pray for those things you desire, speak out words from the Scriptures or based upon the truth of the Scriptures that demonstrate and reinforce your faith.

Faith says, "God's in charge and He is going to work this out for my good, in His timing, using His methods."

Faith says, "I may not see the answer I desire today, but I know Jesus is the Answer, and He will provide all things I need."

Faith says, "I refuse to doubt that God is in full control of the situation. I choose to believe He will work all things together for my good."

Faith says, "God desires my good. He is my Savior, my Lord, and my Rewarder." Hebrews 11:6 tells us this about faith: *"Without faith it is impossible to please Him, for he who comes to God must believe that He is, and that He is a rewarder of those who seek Him."*

Fear and faith cannot operate at the same time. You have been given the choice as to whether you will give in to fear or exercise your faith. Which will it be? Fear or faith?

If faith is present, fear must go away.

Make up your mind to walk in faith and to live by faith. You don't have to remain depressed. You can tell yourself today, "Snap out of it! Get over it! Get on with it!"

You may feel weak, down, or blue on the inside, but speak and pray and believe with strength. The strength will overcome the sadness within you.

Don't let discouragement, dismay, despair, or depression entangle your soul. Move beyond the pain of the past into the joys of the present. With Christ, your best days are yet to come.

11

Moving beyond
a Victim Mind-Set

One of the core causes of depression is a victim mind-set—a belief that you have no power to determine your own choices or to withstand evil that may come against you.

One of the best roles a lot of people know how to play in life is the role of victim. They say, "Bad things just keep happening to me." The truth is, victims always become victimized!

People who live in fear just have more and more things that cause them to be afraid.

People who dwell in a state of worry find they have more and more things to be anxious about.

People who set themselves up to be ridiculed and criticized find that others around them are more than happy to oblige—they just hear more and more ridicule and criticism.

God's Word says that we are *"more than conquerors"* (Rom. 8:37) in Christ Jesus! And what does the Bible say that we have conquered? Tribulation, distress, persecution, famine, nakedness, peril, and the sword (v. 35)! In today's terms, that would be hard times, bad times, unjust times, lacking times, difficult times, and deadly times!

God's position is never that His people see themselves as victims or have a "poor me" attitude. God's position is that His people see themselves as capable, able, and victorious—not because of who we are in our own strength, but because of what He has done for us, is doing in us, and will do on our behalf! We are not *"more than conquerors"* in our own strength or wisdom. We are *"more than conquerors"* in Christ Jesus!

The Israelites had a victim mind-set when they left Egypt. They had been slaves for four hundred years. They were a sorely oppressed people.

One of the main reasons the Lord kept the Israelites wandering in the desert for forty years before they went in to claim the land God had promised to them was so the Israelites would learn how to fight!

You may remember the story. The Israelites had come to the edge of the Promised Land within a relatively short period of time after leaving Egypt. Moses had sent twelve men—each man a leader in his tribe—to spy out the land and determine how best to conquer it. The leaders came back reporting that the land *"certainly does flow with milk and honey"* (Num. 13:27). They showed the people some of the abundance of fruit they had picked in the land.

Two of the leaders, Caleb and Joshua, were filled with faith that God would do what He had said He would do. They said to the Israelites, *"We should by all means go up and take possession of it, for we shall surely overcome it"* (v. 30). They gave a faith report.

The other ten leaders rose up to give a negative report. They said, *"We are not able to go up against the people, for they are too strong for us"* (v. 31). They reported men of great size and said, *"We became like grasshoppers in our own sight, and so we were in their sight"* (v. 33).

Grasshoppers, not men! That's the way they saw themselves. They had a severe case of victim mind-set, and they instilled fear in the rest of the people. God's Word tells us that the entire congregation of the Israelites *"lifted up their voices and cried, and the people wept that night"* (Num. 14:1).

Never mind that God had said He was going to give them the land. Never mind that God had said, *"I also established My covenant with them, to give them the land of Canaan"* (Exod 6:4). Never mind that God had said,

> *I will take you for My people, and I will be your God, and you shall know that I am the LORD your God, who brought you out from under the burdens of the Egyptians. And I will bring you to the land which I swore to give to Abraham, Isaac, and Jacob, and I will give it to you for a possession; I am the LORD.* (vv. 7–8)

The Israelites were so afraid after the negative report from the ten spies that they began to call for a leader to replace Moses—they were looking for someone to lead them back to Egypt!

In the end, none of those who spoke or believed the negative report lived to set foot in the Land of Promise. Only Caleb and Joshua crossed the Jordan River.

For forty years the Israelites wandered in a desert wilderness. God used that time to build backbone in His people—to build up courage, to teach them how to stand up in faith, and to teach them how to face down their fears and trust God for what He had promised to give them.

God may have you in a wilderness today. You may call it a "slump" or "the blues" or "depression" or a "desert period."

What is God's highest purpose in this time? It's to teach you the same lessons He taught the Israelites. He desires that you learn how to stand up on the inside.

The Sorry State of Those with a Victim Mind-Set

A victim doesn't believe he has any power to make choices. God says otherwise about you and me. He says that we can choose how we will think, feel, or believe in any situation, as well as how we will respond in what we say and do.

A victim doesn't believe he can stand up to an enemy or to an oppressor. God says otherwise. He says we can stand up on the inside and trust God to deal with that enemy or oppressor.

A victim collapses in the face of a challenge. God says you can stand.

A victim becomes paralyzed with fear when faced with a decision. God says you can seek His will, move forward boldly in it, and trust God with all the consequences.

This was not the last time the Israelites resorted to a victim mind-set. When the Philistines came up to challenge the Israelites in the Valley of Elah, King Saul and the men of Israel prepared themselves for war. The Philistines were camped on the hill at one side of the valley, and the Israelites were camped on the opposite hill. For forty days a champion of the armies of the Philistines named Goliath came out and shouted to Saul's army, *"I defy the ranks of Israel this day; give me a man that we may fight together"* (1 Sam. 17:10). The stakes were high—the winner would take control over the land. (See 1 Samuel 17:1–10.)

God's Word tells us, *"When Saul and all Israel heard these words of the Philistine, they were dismayed and greatly afraid"* (v. 11). They cowered in fear. Their hearts melted within them.

David came to the camp to bring provisions to his brothers who were in the army, and when he heard this giant named Goliath shout his daily challenge, David asked, *"Who is this uncircumcised Philistine, that he should taunt the armies of the living God?"* (1 Sam. 17:26). David was eventually brought to King Saul and he said to the king, *"The LORD who delivered me from the paw of the lion and the paw of the bear, He will deliver me from the hand of this Philistine"* (v. 37).

God Has Delivered You in Your Past

Think back over your life. What has God already delivered you from? Consider all that has happened to you. There may be people who are surprised that you aren't dead by now from all the tragedy and trouble you have experienced!

Every Sunday I preach to people who should have died from drug overdoses, from severe physical abuse experienced as a child, from gang fights, from giving birth as young teenagers, from neglect, or from sicknesses they had as babies. At least that's what the world would say.

God has said in their lives, "You will live and not die." And God has prevailed and delivered them from evil so that they are alive today.

What about you? You may not have experienced severe trauma, but how many times can you recall being exposed to evil that didn't touch you? How many "near misses" have you had? How many accidents have you "narrowly avoided?"

God has delivered you in the past. His desire is to deliver you now!

You know the story. In the end David was given permission to take on Goliath. He picked up five smooth stones from the creek that ran through the Valley of Elah, picked up his slingshot, and went out to face Goliath.

The Philistine took one look at skinny little David and he said, *"Am I a dog, that you come to me with sticks?"* (1 Sam. 17:43). Goliath began to curse David by his gods and he said, *"Come to me, and I will give your flesh to the birds of the sky and the beasts of the field"* (v. 44).

Goliath was a bully. He was used to having his own way. He was used to someone cowering and running away when he made threats.

David spoke right back. He said, *"You come to me with a sword, a spear, and a javelin, but I come to you in the name of the Lord of hosts, the God of the armies of Israel, whom you have taunted"* (1 Sam. 17:45).

In what power are you standing up to your situation or circumstance? By what authority are you going to prayer against the enemy of your soul?

Jesus said to His disciples, *"Believe Me"* (John 14:11).

He told them, *"He who believes in Me, the works that I do shall he do also; and greater works than these shall he do; because I go to the Father"* (v. 12).

Jesus promised his disciples, *"Whatever you ask in My name, that will I do, that the Father may be glorified in the Son"* (v. 13).

Further, Jesus said to them, *"If you ask Me anything in My name, I will do it"* (v. 14).

You and I are just as much disciples—followers—of Jesus today. His Word is for us.

Are you believing in Him? Are you speaking and acting in His authority? Are you trusting God to do *"greater works"* through you? Are you asking for the victory you need?

David declared to Goliath,

This day the Lord will deliver you up into my hands, and I will strike you down and remove your head from you. And I will give the dead bodies of the army of the Philistines this day to the birds of the sky and the wild beasts of the earth, that all the earth may know that there is a God in Israel, and that all this assembly may know that the Lord does not deliver by sword or by spear; for the battle is the Lord's and He will give you into our hands. (1 Sam. 17:46–47)

What are you speaking to your depression today? What are you saying to the enemy of your soul who delights in seeing you down, paralyzed, immobile, out of action, silenced, weak, and discouraged?

It's time you rose up on the inside and said, "In the name of Jesus, I speak to you, depression. You need to go! God is delivering me!"

Start prophesying to yourself. "I'm coming out of this thing. I'm moving forward. I'm going to recover and have everything I've lost restored to me!"

Start speaking God's Word to your own ears. Start quoting God's promises and God's principles to your own mind.

Start laying hands on your own head and claiming the healing of your memories and your bad thinking!

I feel certain that Goliath had never had anybody speak to him as David spoke to him that day. But David didn't just speak. He acted. God's Word tells us that David *"ran quickly toward the battle line to meet the Philistine"* (1 Sam. 17:48, emphasis added).

Let me give you a little insight into this battle situation.

Goliath was used to a style of fighting in which he stood still, with a shield in front of him that was held in place by an armor-bearer. He would then use a javelin and spear to reach around the shield and jab his opponent. Given his size, the reach of his arms, his strength, and the tremendous power of his weapons, Goliath had been able to defeat all those who fought using his same style.

A victim mind-set puts up a wall between you and other people. It puts a person into inactivity. It jabs at you from two main directions—from one side come messages that continually reinforce your fear, from the other side come messages that reinforce your doubt that God either can or will provide for you, protect you, heal you, or preserve you. A victim mind-set keeps jabbing at you with fear and doubt until the faith in you is all but killed.

Filled with faith, David came running toward Goliath.

Faith is intended to be in motion. It is intended to be used.

Your deliverance from a victim mind-set requires that you do something. If you've been sleeping your life away, faith requires that you get out of that bed and stay up all day. If you've been sitting in a chair all day, wishing and hoping and crying your life away, faith requires that you get up and get busy. If you've been paralyzed by depression after losing a job, faith requires that you starting filling out some employment applications and knocking on doors to see where God might want you to work next! If you've been wounded by rejection because someone you love has abandoned you, faith requires that you get up, get dressed, and get yourself to church so you can be around God's people and receive their love, encouragement, and support.

Get yourself in motion. Take action. Run toward your depression, and get those stones ready to fly.

What is it that we are to hurl at our victim mind-set? Not literal stones—but God's Word. The faith-promise verses of the Bible are our weapons in spiritual warfare. The Word of God is our offensive weapon. (See Ephesians 6:17.) We are to speak out these verses in our prayers. We are to memorize and repeat them to ourselves all through any given day. We are to keep these verses central in our conversation with others.

Trust God to guide your spoken words of faith directly to the heart of the giant that is threatening to destroy your life. Trust God to cause the depression that has been looming over you to lift completely and never return.

Trust God to turn your pain into gain.

Trust God to turn your scars into stars.

182

See Yourself as a Victor, Not a Victim

The major decision that a person with a victim mind-set must make is this: I will choose to see myself as a victor, not a victim. How you see yourself, how you speak about yourself, and how you identify yourself will determine how you act and, in turn, how others will act toward you.

Merlene was abused horribly as a child. She was repeatedly molested for nearly five years by an uncle who lived just a few houses away from her home. What she experienced with her uncle left her deeply scarred as she entered her teen years. She easily fell into a victim mind-set any time she was around a strong, dominating male figure. The result, of course, was that some of these ungodly men took advantage of her. She was raped several times, although she didn't want to use the word *rape* for what either her uncle or these men did to her. She had developed such a poor image of herself that she believed she deserved what had happened to her and that she was irreparably damaged and of no value as a person because of what she had experienced in her past.

When Merlene came to the Lord, she knew that God had forgiven her of all her sin and that He had cleansed her from all unrighteousness. She knew that what had been done to her had been against her will and that she was not at fault. She knew that she had done nothing to deserve being the victim of incest or rape.

She knew all this in her mind, according to what others said to her and what the Word of God said to her. Yes, she knew it in her mind. But she didn't know it in her heart and in her spirit.

She continued to think about what had happened. She continued to talk about it—not only to a counselor, but to close family members and friends. She didn't just talk it out once or twice or ten times in seeking prayer and help from godly counselors and friends. She continued to think about it and talk about it for fifteen years!

183

One day her beloved grandmother, with whom she lived, said to her, "Listen, child. I've heard that old record. I've heard that record so often it is getting scratchy and on my nerves. I want you to stop talking about what happened to you in the past. You're not a child any longer. You're not a teenager. You're a thirty-four-year-old woman! What happened to you as a little girl and as a teenager happened more than half your life ago. Let it die. Bury it. Plant some flowers on that grave and move on!"

Merlene was deeply hurt. She quietly fussed and fumed for several days about what her grandmother had said to her. Finally she went to her grandmother and said, "Mumma, you don't really care what happened to me. You've just been pretending to care. If you really loved me, you wouldn't mind my talking about what happened to me so I can get it out of my system."

Her grandmother said, "Child, I've heard you talk about how you were molested as a child and raped as a teenager. I've heard all the stories. I've heard every incident. I've heard it and heard it for fifteen years now. It's because I do love you that I'm telling you, it's time for you to stop thinking about this and talking about this. I want to hear you talk about what God is going to do in your future and how He is going to help you and bless you and lead you into great and wonderful things. I want to hear about your dreams and plans and hopes and goals."

Merlene began to sob. "I don't have a future," she said.

"Oh, yes, you do, child," her grandmother replied. "Ask God to show it to you."

"But I don't have any plans or hopes or goals," she moaned.

Her grandmother replied, "Ask God to give you some. Start thinking about what you can do, what you'd like to do, where you'd like to go, how you'd like to live, what you might like to study, what you might like to see or experience or accomplish. Quit thinking and talking about what was—start talking about what might be!"

"I wish all those terrible things had never happened to me."

"So do I, child," her grandmother said. "But as long as you keep thinking and talking about those terrible times, they continue to 'happen' to you. Every time you bring up one of those memories you relive that experience, and each time you relive one of those experiences, you get hurt all over again. Give up thinking you have to hang on to those memories! Give those terrible times to God!"

From that day forward, every time Merlene brought up the past, her grandmother said, "What are you planning to do next week, Merlene? What goals have you set for yourself next month, Merlene? What are you hoping for in your future, Merlene?"

There were times, of course, when Merlene resented and resisted what her grandmother was trying to do—she cried at times in an attempt to get her grandmother's sympathy, she threatened to move out, she got angry, she gave her grandmother the silent treatment. But week by week, month by month, things began to change.

Merlene's grandmother told me not long ago, "Merlene has enrolled in a night course at the local community college. She's starting to make some new friends—the first new friends she's had in a very long time. She's making plans for a little trip as soon as the school year is over. She hasn't mentioned her past to me in more than three weeks—I'm keeping track, pastor!"

"What changes have you seen in her attitude?" I asked.

"She actually laughed out loud last week," her grandmother said. "I've heard her humming to herself while she fixes her breakfast. She is spending a lot of time reading and studying for her night class, so I think her mind is occupied on good things. Overall, she seems much happier than she was this time six months ago. She's got some goals. She finally sees that God has a future for her."

God's Word tells us, *"Behold, the ships also, though they are so great and are driven by strong winds, are still directed by a very small rudder, wherever the inclination of the pilot desires. So also the tongue is a small part of the body"* (James 3:4–5).

What you think about—and what you talk about—sets the course for your future. As long as you think and talk about the hurts of your past, the ship of your life is going to go round and round, never moving forward, and if anything, drifting back toward the rough seas you've known in the past.

Start thinking and talking about the good future God has planned for you. Get the ship of your life moving in the right direction!

Stop thinking about your former girlfriend, who cheated on you and left you for another man.

Stop dwelling on that former boyfriend, who took all your money and ran off with another woman.

Stop reminding yourself of that former boss, who filled your days with criticism and angry demands.

Stop reminding yourself of all the times you've been treated unfairly.

Stop bringing to your remembrance all the times you've been hurt.

Merlene's grandmother had some good advice: "Let those bad memories die. Bury them. Plant some flowers on those graves and move on!"

12

Moving beyond
Failed Relationships

Wes lived in the shadow of a failed relationship for nearly fifteen years. His wife, Lorette, had walked out on him for another man—actually, it was her boss. She had been a receptionist in a dental clinic, and she left Wes to move in with the dentist for whom she worked. The relationship didn't last. But when Lorette returned to Wes two years later in hopes of reconciling their relationship, Wes realized she wasn't really serious about reconciling and that he couldn't trust her. He told her he didn't want to jump right back into living together, and he was wise to say that. Within ten weeks, Lorette was dating someone else, whom she later married.

Wes was shattered the first time Lorette left him. He was almost equally shattered when she came back and so quickly left again. In his pain, he vowed never to date again, and for fifteen years he didn't.

During those years, Wes worked long hours at his job and received several promotions. He got very involved in church work on weekends and was especially active in the men's group helping to remodel and repair homes for elderly people in the congregation. But Wes didn't date.

Then he went on a retreat that dealt with relationships and especially the topic of "How to Deal with Rejection." He was deeply troubled by what he heard in that seminar. He went to a pastor I know and said, "I thought I was over Lorette and healed of that divorce, but suddenly I found myself on the brink of tears all over again. Obviously I didn't deal with something. What more can I do? I've done my best to forgive her. I've tried not to hate her or feel anger toward her."

The pastor said, "But did you deal with rejection? Did you deal with the fact that the ship named Loretta sailed out of your harbor and is never coming back?"

"I guess not," Wes said. "I know it sounds crazy, but I guess in some way I've been hoping that she'd realize all she lost and come back and settle down for good."

Once Wes realized what was really happening in his life, things changed for him. He asked the Lord to heal him of the wounds of rejection he was feeling. And you guessed it: Within six months he was dating, and within a year he was married to a lovely woman who is now the mother of his daughter.

In the aftermath of a failed relationship, the immediate feelings are often ones of hurt, anger, and hate. The lingering feeling may be one of bitterness if injustice or unfairness was involved. But the prevailing emotion that can tie a person up and cause a person to be kept off-balance in the long run is nearly always rejection. Before you can live in total emotional freedom, you are going to have to face up to all these emotions that can occur in the wake of a failed relationship.

The Core Issues Associated with a Failed Relationship

Hurt, rejection, anger, hatred, and bitterness are all emotions that are related to a "failure" in a relationship.

Stop to think about it for a moment. Any hurt you feel deep inside is linked in some way to another person. If the hurt is deep, there's nearly always an element of rejection involved—plain and simple, we aren't hurt by people who don't matter to us. If a stranger walks up to you and says, "I don't want anything to do with you," you might scratch your head in puzzlement, but you won't feel hurt. You didn't have anything to do with that person in the first place, so what does it matter if that person doesn't want anything to do with you? We are emotionally wounded only by those we admire, desire, respect, love, like, or in some way want to be in relationship with. And, in the vast majority of cases, the hurt we feel is rooted in a feeling that the person is rejecting us, pushing us away, or in some way distancing himself or herself from us.

Any deep anger that you harbor in your heart is related to what you believe somebody—or some group of people—did to you or said about you. It may have been something another person did to you long ago. It may be something another person did or said just a few minutes ago. Anger is always rooted ultimately in something we perceive to be a lie or a sin against us. You can't really be angry with a person who tells you the truth with a desire to see you experience all God wants to give you or create in you. Oh, you may be angry for a moment, but if you truly are a follower of the Lord, you ultimately will be thankful to God and to that person for speaking the truth to you in love.

At the core of real deep-seated, long-standing anger is a feeling that an injustice of some kind was done. Something was said that should not have been said. Something was done that violated God's commandments related to kindness and goodness and justice. Something was done that amounts to a trespass on your soul or sin against you.

Hatred and bitterness flow from unresolved anger and hurt. If anger and hurt, including feelings of rejection, are allowed to sink deep into the heart and smolder there, deep feelings of hatred may develop. Those feelings are likely to include feelings of distrust and suspicion. They may be manifested in various forms of cruelty, abuse, slander, or gossip.

If anger is allowed to smolder within our hearts, eventually we are going to feel bitter. What happens is this: The feelings related to injustice that caused us to feel angry in the first place will continue to cry out for justice. The longer we don't receive the justice we think we deserve, the greater our bitterness will grow. We will feel put upon and downtrodden.

The end result of this brew of hurt, rejection, anger, hatred, and bitterness in the human heart is misery—deep, troubling, anxiety-ridden misery!

And it all begins when a relationship fails.

If we truly are going to overcome painful emotional wounds—hurt, rejection, anger, hatred, and bitterness—we need to face the fact that we have experienced a failed relationship.

Examine What *Really* Happened

To truly walk in freedom after a failed relationship, you first need to ask and answer the question, "What really happened?" Don't be too quick in assuming that you know the answer.

"Well, it's obvious," you may say. "My husband left me for another woman. The failed relationship is with my husband, and it failed because he was unfaithful."

Look deeper. The real core of the failure may be your relationship with your father. Or perhaps your husband's failed relationship with his mother, or his father. Ultimately, there was a failure involved in your relationship or your husband's relationship with God. Get to the core of the relationship that has failed or is failing.

Get to the core issue that drove you apart. It probably wasn't an issue at the surface level of your behavior. Leaving the cap off the toothpaste or overspending the family budget isn't usually the real reason for a failed relationship. The real

190

issue is usually one that runs much deeper and deals with our basic needs for approval, appreciation, love, and respect.

Examine What You Want Now

Then, ask and answer, "What do I really want to happen now?" You are going to have to evaluate whether you truly want the failed relationship to be healed or restored.

"Of course," you may say, "I want my marriage to work." "I want to have friends." "I want to succeed at this job."

Do you really? Recognize that healing and restoration take effort. To heal a damaged, broken, failed relationship is going to take considerable effort on your part. It very likely is going to take patience and persistence over time. It is going to take an increase of faith on your part. It is going to take some heart-to-heart communication and some giving on your part—even when you don't feel like communicating or giving.

Count the cost of healing and restoring what is broken.

Now, I'm not saying that you should just give up and walk away from a relationship that shows signs of failure. Not at all! A marriage is worth fighting for. Your relationship with your children is worth tremendous effort and time. A long-standing friendship is worth healing.

What I'm calling for is your evaluation of what is going to be required on your part—not on the other person's part or even on God's part.

Some people want a failed relationship to be healed in an instant. They expect a "spontaneous miracle" to occur in which everything is suddenly going to be set in order and work perfectly. That may happen, but I've never seen it happen, and I've never heard of it happening, at least not in situations that are reported honestly and accurately. A good relationship takes time and energy and effort to build. The healing of a relationship also takes time and energy and effort.

191

Some people expect the "other person" in the failed relationship to do all the work, all the changing, all the apologizing, or all the giving. That is never what God requires. Both people are going to have to be willing to go to God and ask, "What can I do that I didn't do? What should I stop doing that I've been doing? What needs to be changed in my attitude, my communication patterns, or my habits? What do I need to face up to, own up to, or confess to the Lord? What is my part in the breakdown of the relationship?"

Those are tough questions to ask, tough questions to answer, but vital questions to wrestle with if a relationship is going to be healed.

Why Do Most Relationships Fail?

If we are going to learn how to overcome the hurt and rejection associated with a failed relationship, one of the foremost things we need to face is the primary reason that the relationship failed in the first place.

There are three basic reasons that people who are in love fall out of love, people who are falling in love don't continue to fall in love and part ways, or people who are friends stop being friends.

Now, I'm not talking about relationships that are ill-founded from the beginning. Some relationships are never meant to be, and those relationships are doomed to failure or great heartache from the start.

God spells out the warnings very clearly.

Believers are not to marry unbelievers. If a saint starts a relationship with a sinner, there's going to be conflict because the two people are moving in opposite directions. One is sliding toward hell, and the other is walking toward heaven. One is giving in to the dictates of the flesh, and the other is seeking to follow the impulses of the Holy Spirit. One is pursuing the goals and systems of this world, and the other is seeking to live according to God's commandments and promises. Oil and water don't mix—and neither do relationships in which one person is following Jesus as Savior and Lord and the other isn't.

Being Equally Yoked Is Vital

It takes two people to live in harmony in the relationship I've just described above. Both the husband and wife need to recognize God's model and seek to live it out in their lives.

When a husband leads and a wife is yielding to his leadership, a marriage has a wonderful potential to be strong and to give joy to both spouses. That marriage creates an environment in which children thrive—they feel secure, they feel loved, and they feel God.

When the relationship is not in proper order, however, there's nearly always a huge element of misery and sadness in the marriage and in the family as a whole.

A Christian woman cannot trust an ungodly man to provide for her or give her the sense of security she needs. She is going to feel frustrated, insecure, and deeply troubled in her spirit. A Christian man cannot expect an ungodly woman to yield to him and encourage him and pray for him. He is going to have a deep feeling of loneliness and bitterness that he isn't being respected and loved in the ways he desires to be respected and loved.

The Bible makes it very clear that a husband and wife are to be equally yoked. Only then can they pull together and raise up children who will love and serve the Lord.

If a man and woman are not equally yoked, they each are going to have a significant amount of frustration. When that spouse disappoints, and sometimes disappears, there's going to be a great feeling of rejection, and likely anger, bitterness, and hatred.

The Pride Factor

Self-centered people make lousy friends and marriage partners. People who are so wrapped up in "me, myself, and I" aren't giving people. And trust me on this, any good relationship—friendship, romance, or marriage—requires that both people be givers. Each person must be willing to give ideas, as well as receive ideas. Each person must be willing to give or express emotions, without using emotions to manipulate or control. Each person must be willing to give prayers, time, attention, and material blessings to the other. A stingy, selfish, self-focused person is a *taker,* and people who only take but never give cannot sustain a good relationship.

Let me add this: A good relationship or good marriage is not a fifty-fifty deal. A good relationship requires that each person be willing to give 100 percent of what God requires, not just some of the time, but *all* the time.

If a relationship that was going someplace suddenly comes to a dead end, there's great likelihood that one or both people in that relationship allowed pride to rear its ugly head and assume control. Self rose to the forefront.

Perhaps the most blatant manifestation of pride in a relationship is when one person simply walks away and abandons the marriage or friendship. The person says, in effect, "I want what I want. I'm leaving. I don't care how you feel or what you want. I'm going my way to do what I want to do."

If you believe pride is at work, you need to confront it. You need to ask the other person in your relationship, "Do you want this relationship to succeed? If you do, you are going to have to factor me into the relationship. Relationships take time and effort and give-and-take. I'm willing to do my part. Are you willing to do your part?"

If you desired for a relationship to continue or grow, and the other person said, "I'm outta here," you need to face the fact that there was nothing you could have done to make that person stay. Pride had taken hold.

Go to God and say, "Heal my broken heart. Keep me from becoming bitter or angry or filled with hate. Make my heart soft toward you and toward other people."

And then, don't waste your time mourning for that lost relationship. Get busy doing what it is that God shows you to do.

Sin Factors

In many cases, a relationship fails because of sin on the part of one or both persons in the relationship. The sin may be adultery or fornication. It might also be the opposite—the sin of withholding sex, affection, or words of encouragement from a marriage relationship in order to manipulate or control the other person.

Sexual sins aren't the only sins that can destroy a relationship. The sin may be lying, cheating, or abusing a chemical substance. The sin may be some type of physical or emotional abuse.

Sin always destroys. That's its nature. It always puts something to "death"—it may be the death of affection, the death of respect, the death of trust. In the end, sin always has the capacity to put the relationship to death.

If sin has erupted in your marriage, you need to confront it. Don't sweep it under the rug. Say to the other person in the relationship, "I believe in following the commandments of God. I believe that when a person doesn't follow the commandments, there are consequences to pay—and they aren't good ones. I'm willing to forgive you, but I want to know—are you seeking God's forgiveness? Do you want my forgiveness? Are you going to repent and seek God's way instead of your way and ask God to help you turn away from this sin?"

If the other person in the relationship refuses to face up to the sin, has no interest in seeking God's forgiveness or your forgiveness, and doesn't desire to change, it is difficult to keep the relationship together. When one person is pursuing righteousness and the other person is pursuing sin, they are going in opposite directions.

Refuse to go along with the sin of the other person. Don't say, "Well, for the sake of the relationship, I'll join in the sinning." Refuse to compromise your stand for Christ Jesus.

God will honor your faithfulness to Him. Ask Him to heal your own heart and to forgive you for any way in which you may have allowed sin in your home. And then, ask the Lord to give you the strength to trust Him to provide for you and lead you and to show you exactly what He would have you do.

I'm certainly not saying that you should bail out of a relationship at the first sign of sin in your spouse or in a friend. We are all sinners. None of us is ever in a relationship with a perfect person—for that matter, your spouse and your friends are stuck with your imperfections, too! But there are patterns of sin and habits of sinning that can develop to the detriment of one or more people involved in the relationship or family. At times you will need to separate yourself from the sin for your own protection and preservation, or for the protection and preservation of your children.

Any time a believer walks away from sin and refuses to participate in it, even as a silent, "consenting" partner, God will honor that response to sin and help the person who has the courage to walk away.

Ask God to heal your broken heart and to keep you from bearing any false guilt.

A Failure to Follow God's "Order" of Authority

In this area, we aren't talking about friendships, but rather relationships in which there is an established order of authority according to God's Word. In a friendship, two people can give and receive from each other on pretty much an equal footing.

When it comes to an employer-employee relationship, however, a chain of command is in effect. God has provided an order of authority for that particular relationship. In the Bible, we don't find the words *employer* or *employee,* but rather *master* and *servant.* Servants are always subject to their masters. They are to obey their masters and do their work cheerfully, willingingly, and to the best of their ability and strength. Masters are to treat their servants generously, kindly, and with respect.

As another example, those in political authority and those who are subject to them are in a chain-of-command relationship. Those who are in spiritual authority in the church and those who are subject to them are also in this type of relationship. Those who are in leadership are to lead with wisdom, compassion, and according to the commandments and statutes of God. Those who are "subject" are to pray for those in leadership over them, to obey God's commandments, and to keep the laws that have been prescribed (to the extent that those laws do not require a person to break any of God's laws).

These rules for order of authority in a relationship are set out very plainly in God's Word. We live in peace when we follow God's chain of authority; we experience conflict when we don't.

Perhaps the most troublesome of all chain-of-command relationships for us is the order of authority God has set out for a marriage and a family. We need to be very clear on what it is that God requires of each person in a marriage if we are going to fully understand why many marriages are in trouble or are failing today.

God's Prescribed Roles in Marriage

This is not a book specifically on marriage, but let me remind you of several very important biblical principles related to marriage.

God has called every husband to be the spiritual head of his house. A great many men, however, see themselves primarily as a breadwinner, and they leave the spiritual matters of a family to their wives. The truth of God's Word is that every husband and father is called by God to speak the Word of God to his family every day, to rise up every day and pray for his family, and to lead the family in keeping the commandments of God.

God has called every wife to provide prayer support and encouragement to her husband. A great many women, however, do not trust their husbands to take the lead, and they refuse to yield spiritual authority to their husbands.

I believe it takes a great deal more courage and faith for a woman to enter into a marriage relationship than for a man. A woman is putting herself into a situation in which God calls her to yield her will and her desires to those of her husband. Prior to marriage, a woman must yield those desires only to the Lord—she is called to do what He directs, authorizes, plans, prepares, and calls her to do. After marriage, a woman is called by God to yield her will and her desires to her husband, who, in turn, is called to lead His family as God directs him and authorizes him. She's dealing with an unknown quantity—she doesn't know with certainty that her husband is going to be willing to yield himself to the Lord. There's a lot of faith required for a woman to say to herself and to God and to her husband, "I am willing to yield what I want to what God shows you is best for our family. I am willing to yield what I desire to what God reveals to you is His plan for us."

You'll notice that I use the word *yield* instead of *submit*. That's what *submit* means. It doesn't mean that a woman lays down and becomes a doormat for her husband to abuse. No, it's more like two cars showing up at an intersection, and one car must yield to the other or a crash is going to occur. And isn't that what happens? When a wife refuses to yield decision-making or choice-making authority to her husband or when a wife refuses to follow the lead of her husband in making decisions regarding the spiritual atmosphere of the home, crashes occur. And sometimes those conflicts are very serious and can lead to great injury to all parties involved.

The truth of God's Word is that when we get ourselves out of God's order for authority and we take on roles that are outside God's authorization for harmony in the home, we should not be surprised when a marriage gets into trouble or a family relationship fails.

A Word to Wives

Some women know more than their husbands about the things of the Lord, and it takes a great deal of patience and real control of their tongues to say, "I will allow God to work in his life. I will trust God to speak to him, direct him, reveal Himself to him, and teach him."

Some women have more ambition or a stronger will than their husbands, and it takes a great deal of generosity and graciousness for them to say, "I will trust my husband to take the lead in this area of our life together."

Some women are smarter than their husbands, and it takes a great deal of humility for them to say, "I will give my husband all the input and words of wisdom that I can, but, in the end, I will allow my husband to make the final decision."

When a woman will do things the way God desires, the blessings to her are tremendous. God will honor her patience, self-control, generosity, graciousness, and humility in yielding to her husband. He will bless her—sometimes through what

199

He prompts her husband to do, and sometimes in spite of what her husband does.

When a wife yields to her husband, she is saying to the Lord, "I trust You. I may feel hurt, I may feel slighted, I may feel used, I may feel confused at times, but I trust You in this. I will obey You. I am relying on You to honor my obedience and take care of me and my family according to the provisions and promises of Your Word."

I have met women who have said to me, "I'll yield to my husband when he gets right with God." The truth is, when a woman will yield to her husband, there's a much greater likelihood that he *will* get right with God! A wife is called to pray for, support, encourage, and build up her husband, even as she carries out the authority her husband has given to her in helping him pray for, teach, and discipline their children.

Nothing Weak about a Godly Wife!

Many women and a good many men seem to think that being a "yielding wife" means being a weak, unintelligent, unaccomplished, emotionally dependent person. That isn't at all the picture the Bible presents. Go to Proverbs 31 and read what God sets out as the ideal wife:

The heart of her husband trusts in her, and he will have no lack of gain. She does him good and not evil all the days of her life. She looks for wool and flax, and works with her hands in delight. She is like merchant ships; she brings her food from afar. She rises also while it is still night, and gives food to her household, and portions to her maidens. She considers a field and buys it; from her earnings she plants a vineyard. She girds herself with strength, and makes her arms strong. She senses that her gain is good; her lamp does not go out at night. She stretches out her hands to the distaff, and her hands grasp the spindle. She extends her hand to the poor; and stretches out her hands to the needy. She is not afraid of the snow for her household, for all her household are clothed with scarlet. She makes coverings for herself; her clothing is fine linen and purple. Her husband is known in the gates, when he sits among the elders of the land. She makes linen garments and sells them, and supplies belts to the tradesmen. Strength and dignity are her clothing, and she smiles at the future. She opens her mouth in wisdom, and the teaching of kindness is on her tongue. She looks well to the ways of her household, and does not eat the bread of idleness. Her children rise up and bless her; her husband also, and he praises her, saying: "Many daughters have done nobly, But you excel them all."

(Prov. 31:11–29)

This is a strong woman! She has excellent managerial skills and time-management skills. She knows how to provide for her children and her servants. She works long hours. She has a business of her own and knows how to make wise investments from her earnings. She is good at trading and shopping and knows how to clothe her family with style. She knows how to plan in advance. She's highly intelligent and not at all afraid to speak her mind. This woman is nobody's doormat!

But notice, too, that she does her husband *"good and not evil."* Her husband trusts in her. He knows he has her respect, her support, her encouragement. He knows that when decision-making time comes, she will yield to him and that in all matters of "authority" she will follow his leadership.

In order to be this kind of wife, a woman needs to know that she can trust her husband and rely upon him to provide for her and her children. A wife has a much greater need for security than a husband. She needs to know that her "nest" is secure and that her children are safe.

Problems with leadership in the family can manifest themselves in various ways. Some families are in trouble because the wife is trying to lead. Some families are in trouble because the husband is refusing to take the leadership role God has set before him.

God has called the husband to lead the team called "family." He has called the wife to be the support system for the husband. And He has called children to obey and learn from their parents.

A Word to Husbands

Husbands, you need to come to grips with the truth that God requires you to do some yielding, too.

Everything I just wrote to wives is applicable to you except that you need to yield to the Lord Himself.

Your desire as a man with a strong ego and a strong will is going to be to take charge and to have an attitude, "I rule. I know what's best." It takes a great deal of humility to say to the Lord, "I will do what You want me to do. I will obey You. I will trust You to speak to me, direct me, and show me how you want me to live in relationship with my wife and children."

Your ambition and your will are going to be called into submission by the Lord. It will take faith on your part to say to the Lord, "Not my dreams, but Your dreams. Not my desires, but Your desires. Not my will, but Your will." God will call you to yield to His commandments, His principles, His plans.

One of the things that the Lord is going to reveal to you is that you must love your wife as you love your own body—which means you will take care of her and treat her with respect and tenderness and compassion. No sane man inflicts wounds upon himself, either physically or emotionally. Every sane man desires to be shown consideration, kindness, and to receive "TLC"—tender, loving care. Every man wants to be loved and appreciated. God calls and commands husbands to do these very things for his wife—to respect her, treat her tenderly, provide for her, and show her consideration, kindness, and compassion.

When a husband will do things the way God desires, he'll find that God blesses him with a good marriage and a happy home. He'll find great success in all other areas of his life because his prayers are answered, and because, through his obedience to God, he is in the right position to receive *all* the blessings God has for him. God always honors obedience. He always blesses those who live in accordance with His commandments and who diligently pursue His will.

When a husband yields to the Lord, he is saying, "I trust You. I trust You to help me provide for my family. I trust You to help me show love to my family. I trust You to help me be vulnerable in areas I would prefer not to be vulnerable, and to give me the courage to communicate kindness and tenderness to my wife and children. I'm trusting You to honor my obedience."

Traits of Leadership God Blesses

What does it mean for a husband to lead his family in a godly fashion? What does it mean for a leader of any organization to lead in a godly manner?

Although I touched on these basic responsibilities briefly, there are six basic responsibilities that God requires of every leader, and particularly of those who are leading a family or church.

1. A Responsibility to Pray. It is the leader who bears the primary responsibility for prayer. It is the husband's responsibility to pray for his family. When a child hears his father pray for him, that child learns how to pray! He learns what it means to be in right relationship with God and what it means to trust God to meet his needs. He learns more about his father's hopes and dreams for his life and for the lives of each member of the family. He sees an example of his father's love for him in action—it is out of love that a father prays for his children. There are no greater lessons than these that a child can learn in developing self-esteem.

203

2. A Responsibility to Share God's Vision. It is the leader who bears the primary responsibility for hearing from God and for relaying God's vision for the family to his wife and children. It is the father who should be saying to his family, "Here's what God has called us to do. Here's how God has called us to give, to minister to others in need, to win souls for Christ." It is the father who should be saying, "Here's how we're going to get out of debt. Here's how we're going to save for a house."

3. A Responsibility to Teach. It is the leader who bears the primary responsibility for teaching his children the Word of God, including the commandments of God, the words of Jesus, the stories of the Bible. Even if a father doesn't think he is qualified to be a "teacher," he certainly can read Bible stories aloud to his children at bedtime, watch Bible-based videos with his children, and ask his children to read a child's version of the Bible back to him. All these opportunities are wonderful ways for a father to teach.

4. A Responsibility to Discipline. It is the leader who bears the primary responsibility for disciplining his children. It is not the husband's responsibility to discipline his wife, which is what too many men try to do. It is his responsibility to discipline his children. This means that it is the father who sets the rules for the family—making it very plain what he expects his children to do and not to do. It is also his responsibility for backing up his wife as she enforces the rules of the family. Very often it is the mother who is at home when a child needs correction. Immediate discipline is often the most effective discipline. But no child should ever have any doubt that Mom is enforcing what Dad has set as the rules for the family.

It is the father's responsibility to say to his family, "We're going to church on Sundays, including Sunday school." It is the father's responsibility to say, "You may go here and you may not go there," and to specify whom a child may go with and what time that child is to be home.

5. A Responsibility to Set the Tone or the Atmosphere. It is the leader's responsibility to set a tone of love and courtesy and open communication in the family. If Dad is cold, aloof, distant, silent, and never shows affection, he will find that every member of his family becomes just like him! It is the father who needs to take the lead in praising the good efforts and notable achievements of his wife and children, of teaching politeness and manners, and of showing respect for each family member.

6. A Responsibility to Provide for His Family. Finally, it is the leader's responsibility to provide physically and materially for his family. It is the father's responsibility to put food on the table and a roof over the heads of his wife and children. It is the father's responsibility to make sure his children are safe, protected, and have their basic needs met. This doesn't mean that Dad needs to provide for a child's every want—but rather for his child's basic needs. It is the father's responsibility to work, not to the point that he never sees his wife and children, but to the point that he is able to meet the material and financial needs of his family.

Let me remind you again of what God's Word says to you as the leader of your family:

> *You husbands likewise, live with your wives in an understanding way, as with a weaker vessel, since she is a woman; and grant her honor as a fellow heir of the grace of life, so that our prayers may not be hindered. To sum up, let all be harmonious, sympathetic, brotherly, kindhearted, and humble in spirit; not returning evil for evil, or insult for insult, but giving a blessing instead; for you were called for the very purpose that you might inherit a blessing. For* "LET HIM WHO MEANS TO LOVE LIFE AND SEE GOOD DAYS REFRAIN HIS TONGUE FROM EVIL AND HIS LIPS FROM SPEAKING GUILE. AND LET HIM TURN AWAY FROM EVIL AND DO GOOD; LET HIM SEEK PEACE AND PURSUE IT. FOR THE EYES OF THE LORD

ARE UPON THE RIGHTEOUS, AND HIS EARS ATTEND TO THEIR PRAYER, BUT THE FACE OF THE LORD IS AGAINST THOSE WHO DO EVIL. (1 Pet. 3:7–12)

Be Cautious in the Relationships You Build

The best way to be free of rejection—as well as to be free of anger, hate, rebellion, and bitterness—is to be very cautious in the relationships you develop! Prevention is worth far more than any plan for a "cure" of relationship troubles.

Certainly you didn't have the privilege of choosing your parents or your siblings. You were born into a family, and you are going to have to deal to some degree with the failures of your mother and father and siblings.

You can, however, choose who you will have as friends.

You can choose the person you will marry.

You can choose how you will treat your own children.

You can choose the person for whom you will work.

You can choose the people from whom you will learn.

You can choose the people you will call your spiritual leaders.

Be very cautious in deciding whether you should be married. Now, I'm all in favor of marriage, but I also recognize that some people should not get married, at least not until certain desires in them change so they are able to enter into marriage and succeed at it.

When a couple marries, they both give up their independence. They do not give up their individuality. Both partners in a marriage should always have their own personalities, their own likes and dislikes, their own "styles," and their own tastes.

But a person does give up independence. He no longer goes where he wants to go, when he wants to go. She no longer buys whatever she desires. He no longer has "boys' night out." She no longer takes off on a vacation by herself.

When two people marry, God's plan is for them to become one—not only in a sexual union, but also in their goals, their plans, their use of resources, and their overall life together. If you don't want to share with another person—if you don't want to give up some of your time and energy and money—to create a mutual life, if you don't want to factor in another person as you set your goals and make your plans, if you aren't willing to take on the responsibility for another person to the degree that God asks you to take on responsibility for praying for that person, caring for that person, and nurturing that person, don't marry! You'll be miserable. You will be setting yourself up for major heartache.

Be very cautious in deciding when you should marry. Give yourself time to determine the character of the person you are thinking about marrying. Don't rush into a decision to marry—I don't care how loudly your biological clock may be ticking or how eager you are to enter into a sexual relationship with that other person.

Take time to develop a deep friendship with the person you are considering marrying. See how the person relates to other people, including various members of his or her family. See how the person responds to a wide variety of situations and circumstances. See how the person acts within a crisis or when facing a problem or difficult choice.

Look Deep into Character

So many people enter into relationships based upon very superficial appraisals. They like the way the person "looks." They are impressed with the clothes the person wears, the car the person drives or the jewelry on the person's hands or neck.

Look deeper.

207

Does the person really know Jesus Christ as his or her Savior? Is this person seeking to follow Jesus Christ as Lord—obeying what He says to do and freely and genuinely lifting up the name of Jesus in conversations so as to build up other people and express love to them?

Does the person have the character traits of someone who is filled with God's Spirit? Is the person loving, joyful, at peace deep within? Is the person patient and consistently kind? Is there a deep gentleness and goodness in the person? Does the person exhibit self-control? Is he or she faithful in attending church? Are these character traits ones that others see in the person—or are you just so blinded by infatuation that you are the only one who sees his or her goodness? Are these character traits ones that you have seen in operation over time, and in a number of different kinds of situations, including some difficult circumstances or hard times?

Does the person display integrity? Is there an abiding consistency between what the person says he or she believes and the way he or she talks? Does this individual "walk the walk" or just "talk the talk" of being a Christian?

Is the person quick to forgive? Quick to apologize?

Does he or she have an ability to nurture or encourage you?

Is the person a generous giver, or selfish and self-centered?

Does the person take into consideration your thoughts, your feelings, your desires? Does the person treat you with respect, never asking you to do anything that you believe is contrary to God's commandments or His will?

Is the person capable of being loyal through thick and thin?

Is he or she emotionally stable? Is the person easily prone to depression? Does he or she erupt in anger? Is the person perpetually negative, pessimistic, or critical?

Is the person flexible when it comes to making decisions and compromises as circumstances change? Does the person have a desire to continue to learn and grow and develop spiritually?

If the person has children from a previous relationship, see how he or she treats those children. You can never expect someone to treat the children you may have together any better than the way he or she treats the children from a previous relationship.

Above all, look for someone who loves God more than he or she loves any other person. If you find someone who loves God above all else, that person is going to be sensitive to God's correction, and he or she is going to want to have a godly relationship with you.

Ask God for His wisdom. God's Word tells us, *"If any of you lacks wisdom, let him ask of God, who gives to all men generously and without reproach, and it will be given to him"* (James 1:5). If you don't know, don't commit. If you aren't sure, don't proceed. If you don't feel peace, don't make a vow.

Trust God to show you how to be healed of the pain you have felt. Trust God to help you stay out of situations and relationships that are sure to cause you pain in the future!

To live free doesn't mean that you live without attachments to people. It means that your attachments are healthy, not manipulative, and not abusive. It means that your attachments give both persons great freedom to be who God created them to be and to do what God created them to do. It means that your attachments allow you to exercise your faith and offer your praise and give your talents to God's work to the best of your ability and with the fullness of your energy. Anything other than this is a sign that there's something unhealthy and unwise at work.

13

Moving beyond Jealousy

A mother once walked in to find her eleven-year-old daughter lying across her bed with her clothes on, not moving and yet not asleep. She said to her daughter, "I told you to come get your nightgown on so you could go to bed. Why are you just lying here?"

The little girl said, "I just don't have one more change in me."

The mother asked her what she meant by that, and the girl said, "I've been changing all day. I got up this morning and changed out of my nightgown into my school clothes, but I did that three times before I found clean clothes that matched. Then I went to school and I had to change into my cheerleading outfit for the pep rally at noon. After the rally, I had to change back into my regular clothes since we weren't allowed to wear our cheerleading outfits to class. During last period, I had to change into my band uniform for a picture for the yearbook, and then change back into my regular clothes to go to the gym when the final bell rang. Once I got to the gym, I had to change into my soccer clothes for soccer practice. After that, I came home and put on jeans. And now I have to change into my nightgown. I just don't have one more change in me."

Change is tough.

There's no getting around that fact.

There's also no denying that the bigger the change a person needs to make, the harder it is.

The truth of God's Word, however, is that we each are required to change. The moment we accept Jesus as our Savior, a great change process begins in us. Some of the changing is the work of the Holy Spirit in our lives. Some of the changing involves things we have to "put on" and "put off" in our lives.

The person who has received Jesus Christ as Savior and has made a commitment to following Him as Lord has a new goal in his life. His new goal is to "grow up" in Christ and to become like Him in every way possible. We become like Him because we have a walking-and-talking relationship with Him. Growing up in Christ is not a matter of keeping certain rules or following complicated rituals. Growing up in Christ happens as you share your heart with the One who has saved your soul. It happens as you read His Word so you can hear the Lord share His heart with you.

As we grow up into the likeness of Christ Jesus, there are some things in our lives that are supposed to change. The more we walk and talk with Jesus, the more we realize that some aspects of our lives amount to excess baggage. These aspects of our behavior and speech hold us back from becoming all that Christ desires for us to be. They keep us from experiencing all that He has for us to experience and from receiving all that He desires to give to us.

The more sin a person has been into before he or she accepts Christ as Savior, the more baggage that person tends to have. Sin produces baggage—it produces bad ways of thinking and responding to life, it produces bad habits of speaking and behaving, it produces a bad perspective and a bad understanding.

Jesus was the only person who ever lived on this earth who never had any baggage because He never sinned. Every other person, including you and me, has a certain amount of baggage because we were once sinners.

When we come to Christ, we face the challenge of getting rid of that baggage—of changing the way we think, of lightening the load of the way we feel, of dispensing with some of the ways we have responded out of habit, of trading in some of our old bad habits for new godly ones.

Sin isn't just about drugs or sexual immorality or robbing banks or committing murder. The deeper, far more pervasive baggage are the sins of arrogance, pride, or prejudice against someone who is different. Just as serious are the sins of gossip and jealousy.

Jealousy?

Yes, jealousy. God says jealousy is an ugly thing. It's something we are to change. The Bible says,

> *But if you have bitter jealousy and selfish ambition in your heart, do not be arrogant and so lie against the truth. This wisdom is not that which comes down from above, but is earthly, natural, demonic. For where jealousy and selfish ambition exist, there is disorder and every evil thing.*
> (James 3:14–16)

Owning Up to Jealousy

Perhaps the most difficult step in dealing with jealousy and living free of it is facing the fact in the first place that you are living with an abiding emotion of jealousy or envy.

Jealousy often masks itself under different terms. I once heard a man say, "I'm not jealous. I'm just territorial." Another person once told me, "I'm possessive. Don't I have a right to protect what is mine?"

213

Jealousy is wanting something that you don't have, that somebody else does have, and that you think you deserve more than the other person.

Jealousy is manifested when a person gets upset that she doesn't get to sing the solo part and somebody else does. Jealousy is manifested when a person begins to gossip about the pastor because he drives "too nice" a car.

Any time a person is so involved in protecting his turf that he becomes totally self-focused and manipulative of others, that person has moved into jealousy.

A jealous person will sometimes feel competitive about his friends—he won't want his "best friend" to get married, or for him to befriend others. He wants to be the only friend in his life!

A jealous person will sometimes feel competitive with a spouse, sibling, or other family member—he won't want that family member to get more attention. He or she wants to be the center of attention at all times!

Jealousy tends to run rampant in some families. This is especially true if a parent favors one child over another. It can also be true if a person perceives that God has shown favor to one child more than others. That certainly seemed to be what happened in the family of Moses, Aaron, and Miriam. The Bible tells us,

> *Then Miriam and Aaron spoke against Moses because of the Cushite* [Ethiopian] *woman whom he had married (for he had married a Cushite woman): and they said, "Has the LORD indeed spoken only through Moses? Has He not spoken through us as well?" And the LORD heard it....So the anger of the LORD burned against them and He departed.*
> (Num. 12:1–2, 9)

Aaron and Miriam wanted equal footing with Moses. They wanted equal recognition and acclaim. And God said, "Your jealousy is an ugly thing in My eyes."

214

Ask yourself these important questions:

Is there someone about whom you can find *nothing* good to say?

Do you feel a tightening in your throat that keeps you from giving a compliment to another person?

Do you have a lump in your stomach the size of a grape-fruit when you see another person getting the first-place award you worked so hard to achieve?

Do you feel a little angry when you see another person walking down the aisle to get married, even if you didn't want the man she's marrying, or the woman he's marrying?

If so, you need to face the jealousy inside you.

The Negative Effects of a Jealous Heart

God doesn't want jealousy to be part of any Christian's life because jealousy always brings negative results, not only to the church as a whole, but to the individual who is jealous. The foremost negative effects of jealousy are:

A Desire for Revenge or Destruction

Cain was jealous of Abel because God favored Abel's sacrifice over his own.

Joseph's brothers were jealous of Joseph because he seemed to be the favorite child of their father Jacob.

Notice that in each of these cases, those who were jealous eventually sought to destroy their sibling. Cain killed Abel. Joseph's brothers were about to kill him when they hatched a plot to throw him into a pit and wait until an opportune moment to sell him as a slave.

If you don't deal with your jealousy, eventually you will try to destroy the person you envy. Our prisons today are filled with people who did just that—they murdered someone they considered to be a rival. They embezzled, defrauded, or stole from a person they saw as being in competition with them.

Even if you don't resort to violence, bloodshed, or crime, your unchecked jealousy will lead you to seek to destroy the reputation or good name of the person you envy. You will gossip about that person or slander that person in an attempt to destroy any goodwill others may feel toward him.

Insecurity

Jealousy also makes a person feel insecure. I have watched countless people who had a spouse cheat on them in the past. They have a very difficult time trusting another person. Their lack of trust tends to manifest itself in one of two ways. Either they cling very tightly to any person who shows them the least bit of attention, or they refuse to get involved with any person out of fear of being disappointed or rejected again. In their hearts, they feel insecure—they are always looking for signs that somebody is mistreating them, cheating on them, speaking ill of them, or acting disrespectfully toward them.

An Obstacle to Blessings and the Fulfillment of Your Destiny

Jealousy will become a giant obstacle in the flow of God's blessings toward you. It can keep you from fulfilling your destiny in Christ Jesus.

The truth is that God will not bless a jealous heart. He will not honor jealous behavior toward another person. As I stated earlier, jealousy always results in division and disruption, and both are contrary to God's purposes. He will not reward anything contrary to His purposes.

Jealousy will ultimately make you feel depressed. It will cause you to feel troubled and anxious and discouraged.

That certainly happened to King Saul. After Samuel had told him that the kingdom would no longer be his, Saul felt a built-in jealousy that had no real focus. He was jealous of the unknown person who would one day succeed him. He became so agitated in his spirit that those closest to him advised him to seek out a skilled musician who could play soothing music to him on a harp. (See 1 Samuel 16:14–17.)

Why Do People Get Jealous?

There are several things at the root of jealousy, including fear of loss, low self-worth, unmet basic needs, and a competition for God's favor or for status.

Fear of Loss

The jealous person is afraid that he won't get his needs met. The jealous person is afraid that his spouse is going to cheat on him and he will lose the number-one position in her heart, or perhaps even lose his marriage and family. The jealous person is afraid that he is going to lose his job or position or a possession or a relationship.

The jealous person has a very difficult time hearing a compliment given to another person or seeing another person being given a raise, acknowledged with an award, or promoted. The jealous person sees in the advancement of another person a loss of recognition or reward for himself.

Low Self-Worth

The jealous person is likely to look at another person who is prospering or succeeding and say, "He really thinks he's something, doesn't he?" No, in the vast majority of cases the other person doesn't think that at all. It's the jealous person who thinks of himself as nothing.

It is extremely important that you as a believer in Christ Jesus begin to see yourself as an original and beloved creation of God. The Lord made you to be one of a kind. He has a special plan and purpose for your life. He has given you a unique set of talents, personality traits, resources, experiences, skills, and ministry gifts in order to accomplish that plan and purpose. He has a unique place for you to use your talents, and He has a unique timing for your success. Nothing about you will ever be duplicated exactly.

God does not desire for you to be "just like" anybody else. He doesn't desire for you to want what another person has or does.

Stop comparing yourself to others.

The truth is...

There will always be somebody who looks better than you—at least in the eyes of other people.

There will always be somebody who is stronger than you.

There will always be somebody who has more money or more possessions than you.

There will always be somebody smarter than you—at least in some topic or area of expertise.

There will always be somebody who gets more recognition than you—at least in some area of life.

Accept the basics of the way God made you and focus on developing what has been given to you!

We always seem to want what we don't have! Curly-headed people always seem to want straight hair, and straight-haired people seem to want curls. Short people want to be taller, and tall people want to be shorter. Dark-skinned people sometimes want to be lighter-skinned, and lighter-skinned people nearly always to be darker-skinned (at least to the point that they will seek out a tanning booth).

God says, "Accept the way I made you! I made you the way you are for a purpose. Go with My design!"

Now that doesn't at all mean that if we are out of shape we shouldn't try to get in shape. It doesn't mean that we should never use makeup or try to dress well or lose those extra pounds we are carrying around. It does mean that we should accept the basics of our physical creation, personality, culture, race, age, and heritage. Go with what you have been given! Make the most of what you already have!

Unmet Basic Needs

The final core reason for jealousy lies in the area of unmet basic needs. For example, if a woman sees a husband kissing his wife and that woman isn't receiving love or affection in her life, she may very well be jealous of that wife who is getting kissed. If a man knows another man is going home to a loving wife and a home-cooked meal, and he doesn't have anybody at home waiting for him—much less a home-cooked meal—he may very well be jealous.

I remember back to the years when our church was very small, and we were meeting in a little storefront space. It was difficult for some of those who were working alongside me to see the buildings, equipment, facilities, and resources of large churches and not feel jealous. We certainly wanted to have a better music program and more parking and a nicer place for worship. We firmly believed that we would know how to thank and praise God for giving us a bigger building, better equipment, nicer facilities, and more resources. In the interim, we had to fight against jealousy. We had to thank and praise God for what He had provided right then. We had to thank and praise God for giving us a vision, but also for giving us work to do to help bring that vision into reality. We had to discipline ourselves to focus on meeting the present needs of the people attending our small fellowship.

The Three Things Necessary for Overcoming Jealousy

In this experience I just shared above, I've just given you the three things that are absolutely necessary if you are going to overcome a spirit of jealousy!

1. Offer Thanksgiving and Praise. If you feel yourself in any way jealous of what another person has or does, begin to thank God for what He has given to you. Praise Him for being the One who can provide for all your needs. Praise Him for His promises that speak to you of your own good future and prosperous provision. Praise Him for being the only One who can supply your deep inner needs to feel worthy and loved. Praise Him for sending you friends and associates and colleagues who can encourage you and love you as you pursue the vision God has given you for your life.

If you are truly thanking God for what you have and praising God for what He says you will have and will do, you won't have time or energy to focus on what others have or do. The person with a truly thankful heart is not a person prone to jealousy.

2. Work toward the Goal God Has Given You. The jealous person can waste an incredible amount of time and energy trying to undermine the person he has set up to be his rival. Use that time and energy to work at the tasks God has given you. Engage in positive, constructive efforts to reach the goal God has set before you. The more you are engaged in hard work, the less you will feel like spending time and energy directed at bringing down your competitors.

A businessman once told me, "I don't waste any resources on trying to bring down my competitors. I spend all my time making a better product and providing a better service to win new clients and keep the old ones happy. If I spend my time that way, my business grows! The fact is, jealousy toward a competitor is a waste of time and emotion. It doesn't produce any new business."

Politicians are slow to learn this lesson, but those who have learned it tend to be very successful. If a politician will tell people what he is going to do, rather than drag down his opponent with personal attacks, that politician is much more likely to gain the respect of the voters, and, in a great many cases, respect is translated into votes.

3. Serve Somebody. Jealousy is rooted to a great extent in an "I want," "I've got to have," "I desire" attitude. The focus is on meeting the needs of self. One of the best antidotes for jealousy is to begin serving others. Reach out to those in need.

You don't need to look far to find somebody who has a need. Visit the sick. Feed the homeless. Work in the shelter for abused women and children. Tutor a child who is behind in school. Help care for the elderly parent of a friend so that friend can get some needed chores and errands done.

Get involved in an outreach ministry of your church. Recognize that all the opportunities to serve within the church are going to be opportunities to give something of yourself to somebody who has a need. Sing in the choir. Teach Sunday school. Usher or park cars. You will be meeting a need!

One of the foremost ways you can serve other people is to help build them up spiritually and emotionally. Pray for other people. Speak positive words to them about yourself and about your community or church as a whole. Do your best to build up their faith and help them trust God for healing and wholeness in their lives.

Those who are intent on serving others rarely get jealous.

Begin to Bless the Person You Envy

There was one more thing that God required of us when we were in those small storefront days of our church. He directed me to begin to bless another pastor in our city who had a large, well-established church and who seemingly had no needs.

Don't be surprised if God requires you to do something helpful, beneficial, or "extra nice" for the very person you envy. That's one of God's foremost methods for rooting jealousy out of your heart!

I discovered that this pastor needed some sound equipment. Well, the fact was, I needed some sound equipment for our church—but I knew that the Lord had directed me to buy some sound equipment for him first.

The Lord also directed me to begin to pray for this man, so I began to pray every day for God to bless this pastor. And one day, I discovered as I prayed that I actually meant what I was praying!

That's the way obedience works. We very often begin to obey with our hands and feet and lips and giving, and the feelings come in the wake of the obedience. We make a decision with our minds, we act on that decision in our words and in our deeds, and the feelings of joy and peace eventually come.

If you begin to pray for the person you have envied, and to do good for and to that person, eventually the feeling of jealousy will leave you and in its place, you will feel great joy!

Building Up Yourself as You Build Up Others

Let me point out that if you consistently, constantly, and compassionately do the three things I've suggested above—thank and praise the Lord, engage in old-fashioned hard work aimed at reaching the goal God has given you, and serve other people—you are going to be doing two things simultaneously:

First, you will be creating a stronger, more positive community of people around you. You will be making friends, building up a church fellowship, improving your neighborhood, or creating a stronger family. You will be engaged in activities that bind people together, rather than divide people. You will be involved in ministry that heals and unifies, rather than tears down or disrupts. Those who develop a strong group of friends and loved ones have little need to compete with others.

222

Second, as you become part of a group of believers who are thanking and praising God together, working together, and serving together, you are going to begin to feel approval, love, and respect flowing toward you from other members of that group. Something inside you is going to be healed as part of that process. You are going to find that your self-esteem begins to rise—you will have satisfaction and a healthy amount of pride about what you are doing in serving others. You are going to feel wanted. You very likely will begin to see that God's love for you is unconditional and highly personal—He has plenty of love to go around.

What if Others Are Jealous of You?

One of life's basic laws is that if a person is successful at anything, somebody is going to be jealous of that success. I don't care if you clean carpets for a living, sweep swimming pools, or trim trees—if you excel at what you do, there will be a person or a company that will try to bad-mouth you or tear you down because you excel.

As long as you stay "average," you won't have that problem. But God never calls His people to be just average. His desire is that we excel in all things we do, and especially so in the use of our spiritual gifts and the talents we employ for the Gospel.

What should you do if you find that another person is envious of you?

Confront the Problem Positively

At times, the best way you can confront and deal with jealousy is to talk about it openly with the person who is expressing envy against you.

If your spouse is jealous, sit down and talk to him or her about the jealousy. Find out what is making your spouse feel insecure. Find out why he or she fears your rejection or feels in competition for your love.

223

If someone has set himself up to always be in competition with you, make an appointment with that person and talk about what is happening between you. Let the person know that you do not want to be at odds with him.

Pray for the Person

Pray against the competitive spirit that seems to have arisen between you and the other person. Pray also that God will have mercy on the person who is jealous.

In the case of Miriam and Aaron speaking against Moses, both Miriam and Aaron experienced very grave consequences at the hand of God on account of their jealousy. Miriam was struck with leprosy, and Aaron was struck with shame and remorse at her condition.

For his part, Moses prayed for Miriam, *"O God, heal her"* (Num. 12:13).

Moses did not harbor resentment against Aaron and Miriam for their jealousy. He continued to trust them and treat them well. He continued to include them in ministry functions as leaders among the Israelites. He never spoke out against them before the people.

If someone has expressed jealousy toward you—even to the point of speaking ill of you—recognize that God knows all about their words, their actions, and the attitude of their hearts. Trust God to deal with them. Forgive them in your own heart. And then, pray that God will be merciful to them and forgive them. For them to continue to be jealous will only create greater havoc in your life—it will be far better for you if they turn from their jealousy and experience God's love and forgiveness!

King Saul: A Case Study in Selfish Ambition and Jealousy

In many cases, a person who is jealous of others is also a person who has an abiding selfish ambition that is just as entangling, manipulative, and destructive as jealousy. This certainly was the case in King Saul.

Saul was God's choice to be the first king of the Israelites. The Lord made it very clear to the prophet Samuel, the last great judge of Israel, that Saul was His chosen servant. For his part, Saul was a reluctant candidate at first, even hiding himself among the luggage carts at the time Samuel sought to reveal him to the people as their king. (See 1 Samuel 10:17–24.)

In the early years of his reign, Saul was a good king. He prophesied among the prophets. (See 1 Samuel 10:1–11.) He rallied the people to fight their enemies. He led the people in providing sacrifices to God and in following the word of the Lord that came through the prophet Samuel.

But the day came when Saul began to have selfish ambition.

Without consulting the Lord—and that is the key point I want you to see—Saul chose three thousand men of Israel to go to war against the Philistines, the enemy people who lived to the south and west of the kingdom of Israel. Two thousand of the men were under his command, and a thousand were under the command of his son Jonathan. This fairly small army struck the Philistine camp at Geba.

Saul didn't know what he had started. He had sought some kind of definitive victory against the Philistines, who often conducted raids into Israel. He no doubt thought he was doing his people a favor and enhancing his own power and prestige as king. Instead, he had only stirred up a hornet's nest.

The Philistines came against Israel with thirty thousand chariots and six thousand soldiers on horses. When the men of Israel saw this vast army of people coming up against them—outnumbering them twelve to one and with horses and iron chariots they didn't have—the Bible tells us that the men of Israel ran and *"hid themselves in caves, in thickets, in cliffs, in cellars, and in pits"* (1 Sam. 13:6). In other words, they hid wherever they could find a place to hide!

Saul saw that panic had overtaken the people. Rather than repent for not seeking the wisdom of God on this matter, rather than seek peace with the advancing enemy, Saul immediately sent for Samuel in hopes that Samuel would tell him the Lord was going to help him out of the crisis he had created.

Saul waited seven days. When Samuel didn't show up at the appointed time that he had said he would be there, the army of Saul began to scatter, so Saul took matters into his own hands.

Again operating out of selfish ambition—a desire to promote self and be number one in the eyes of others—Saul took the burnt offerings and peace offerings that had been gathered together and he offered them to the Lord.

No sooner had he finished doing this than Samuel showed up and asked, *"What have you done?"* (v. 4). Saul said,

> *Because I saw that the people were scattering from me, and that you did not come within the appointed days, and that the Philistines were assembling at Michmash, therefore I said, "Now the Philistines will come down against me at Gilgal, and I have not asked the favor of the LORD." So I forced myself and offered the burnt offering.* (vv. 11–12)

Samuel replied to Saul,

> *You have acted foolishly; you have not kept the commandment of the LORD your God, which He commanded you, for now the LORD would have established your kingdom over Israel forever. But now your kingdom shall not endure.* (vv. 13–14)

In one foolish act of self-promotion and selfish ambition, Saul became a one-term dynasty. He knew from that moment on that none of his heirs would succeed him on the throne. His power and influence would be limited to his own lifetime. That was a cruel blow for any leader of that time.

Saul's selfish ambition didn't stop there.

He built an altar to the Lord and he inquired of God, asking, *"Shall I go down after the Philistines? Wilt Thou give them into the hand of Israel?"* (1 Sam. 14:37).

God did not answer him.

Saul responded to God's silence by seeking to determine for himself why God wasn't answering. He believed that it must be because of sin in the camp, and he sought to uncover that sin. He had made a vow to God that whoever had violated his orders would be killed. But then, when it came to light that the one who had disobeyed, though unknowingly, was Jonathan, Saul was prepared to kill his own son. Because of Jonathan's valor in battle, the Israelites came to his rescue, and his life was spared.

Again and again, Saul made choices that said, "I'm in charge—not God. I'm in charge not only of my life but the lives of my family members and of all those in Israel—not God."

Any time a person assumes that he is in total charge of his life and that he can do whatever it is that he decides to do without any consequences, that person is ruled by selfish ambition. He cannot succeed. The truth is that no person is in total charge of his own life. No person can take one breath beyond what God allows him to take. No person can add one heartbeat to his life beyond what God allows. No person can acquire or keep any material possession, any status in society, any amount of fame, or any position of authority unless God allows that to happen.

The person who has selfish ambition is a person who says, "I can make whatever plans I want to make, and then go to God and ask Him to put His rubber stamp of approval on those plans. I can make whatever decision suits me, and if it turns out to be a sin, I can always go to God and ask Him to forgive me and, in the end, I'll get not only what I want but also God's forgiveness."

227

That's arrogance!

That's pride!

That's selfish ambition to the extreme!

God's desire is for us to seek His will first and foremost and not to act until we know with certainty that we are doing what He has authorized us to do.

Anything that God authorizes us to do is going to be something that can be accomplished without breaking any of His commandments. It is something that can be done with a pure heart. It is something that will be totally in keeping with God's master plan for all mankind—it will be totally within the will of heaven.

When God authorizes us to do something, He will always provide what we need to get the job done. We'll have joy and a sense of eternal purpose in our hearts about the job that lies ahead. We'll have the strength and energy and wisdom to do the job. And we will succeed as we make the effort.

The exact opposite is ultimately the case for all who operate out of selfish ambition.

Those who operate out of selfish ambition break God's commandments—sooner or later. Their hearts are not pure. They do not take into consideration others around them. In the end, their human resources, human strength, and human wisdom fail them. They do not succeed, and they have no joy in what they have undertaken.

That certainly was the case with King Saul.

The more he disobeyed God, the more he failed before God, and the more miserable he became.

The nation of Israel was in nearly constant warfare. Saul received serious rebukes from Samuel, including this word of the Lord: *"I regret that I have made Saul king"* (1 Sam. 15:11).

Samuel came to Saul at last with this admonition and word of judgment:

Behold, to obey is better than sacrifice, and to heed than the fat of rams. For rebellion is as the sin of divination, and insubordination is as iniquity and idolatry. Because you have rejected the word of the LORD, He has also rejected you from being king. (1 Sam. 15:22–23)

It was too late for repentance on Saul's part. Saul confessed that he had sinned and transgressed the command of the Lord, and I have no doubt that God forgave Saul. But the consequences associated with his past sin were in place. Saul was no longer God's choice to rule over Israel.

Note how God saw Saul's selfish ambition. He saw it as rebellion and insubordination.

That's always the status of selfish ambition before the Lord. When we want what we want more than we want what God wants, we are always in rebellion. We are into insubordination.

Note the severity with which God regards selfish ambition. He sees it as being on par with divination, iniquity, and idolatry. (See 1 Samuel 15:23.) These were sins that God called abominations—the most serious and deadly of sins. They were sins that God abhorred.

The Transition to Jealousy

As is nearly always the case, Saul wasn't prone only to selfish ambition. Like most people who are bent on being number one and exalting themselves into the premier position in all situations, Saul was jealous of any other person he perceived to be a threat to his popularity, fame, or position.

He was especially jealous of David. The day came after David killed Goliath that the people who lined the road cried out as David passed, *"Saul has slain his thousands, and David his ten thousands"* (1 Sam. 18:7). The Bible tells us that *"Saul became very angry, for this saying displeased him; and he said, 'They have ascribed to David ten thousands, but to me they have ascribed thousands. Now what more can he have but the kingdom?'"* (1 Sam. 18:7–8). From that day on, Saul regarded David with great suspicion.

King Saul "excelled" in slaying thousands, but David excelled even more in killing ten thousands.

Every time jealousy is allowed to go unchecked and unchallenged, it will cause disorder and division.

From the day Saul allowed jealousy into his heart, he was divided from David. He removed David from his presence and gave him a position with the military, saying, *"My hand shall not be against him, but let the hand of the Philistines be against him"* (v. 17). He then offered David the hand of his daughter Michal in marriage, but the dowry price he set for the marriage was high—a hundred foreskins of Philistine soldiers. Saul thought surely David would be killed in this attempt, or at the very least, fail miserably.

David, however, returned to King Saul with two hundred foreskins. Saul had to allow David to marry his daughter. He became even more jealous of David—in part because his daughter dearly loved David and in part because David's reputation among the people continued to grow until he was *"highly esteemed"* (v. 30) in the land.

Saul began to make direct attempts on David's life—hurling spears at him and sending assassins to kill him. David escaped each time. For nearly a decade, Saul hunted for David in a desire to kill him. He was troubled in his mind about David, nearly consumed with jealousy that turned to hatred.

Jealousy will change a person's demeanor, his attitude, his decisions, his choices, his behavior. We sometimes call jealousy "the green-eyed monster," and that's what it is—a monster that takes root in a person's mind until the person becomes a monster in the way he treats other people. Jealousy is an ugly thing.

Those who are consumed with jealousy think nothing of lying about the person they feel jealousy toward. They think nothing of spreading malicious rumors.

God never honors jealousy in a Christian's heart. We must give no place to jealousy about the way other people look, the jobs they have, the family life they have, or the ministry God has given them.

If self-centered ambition is filling your heart today...

If jealousy is the norm for you...

Take action! You are not living in freedom. You are still in bondage to the one who seeks your destruction. Break free, and then choose to live free.

14

Moving beyond
a Spirit of Failure

No person is ever so successful that he or she won't experience a time of failure or a setback. At times, that failure may come as a result of doing what is right before God.

There's no doubt about it—if you are living a genuinely godly life, there's somebody who has been in your life, is in your life now, or who will be in your life who will seek to destroy you. Every righteous person faces detractors and persecutors and denouncers and critics at some time. Why? Because the devil can't stand our relationship with God, and he can't tolerate your godly life. He will put an intent of evil into the heart of some person to attack you and attempt to do you in. That person may not kill you physically, but that enemy who has become a tool of the devil most assuredly will seek to defame your reputation, harm your marriage, weaken your financial holdings and business, interfere with your relationship with your children, or ruin some other aspect of your life. The devil's goal is ultimately to destroy your relationship with the Lord.

It doesn't matter how godly you are. In fact, the more godly you are, the more the devil will attempt to bring you down.

When Does Failure Become a Spirit of Failure?

Not all experiences of failure produce a spirit of failure.

A person can fail at a task or a business or a subject in school or in a marriage or a job. That doesn't mean, however, that the person automatically has to develop a mind-set, a perspective, or an attitude of failure.

Athletes who compete in sports all lose at some point. Nobody I've ever heard about has a perfect record. Even the best ballplayers and the most proficient track and field stars have lost on occasion. Every athlete I've ever read about has had a "slump" or two in his or her career.

That doesn't mean an athlete develops a spirit of failure. In most cases, the spirit that develops is quite the opposite. There's a spirit of determination, a spirit of believing, a spirit of starting over or doing better that kicks in.

No politician wins all the votes, unless the election is rigged or there is tremendous fear or pressure exerted by a dictator. Does a politician who wins by a margin of 51 percent to 49 percent think of himself as a loser because 49 percent of the people didn't vote for him? No, he thinks of himself as a winner!

No actor gets all the parts.

No business person gets all the contracts.

No salesman makes all the sales.

No student—not even an A+ student—gets all the answers correct on all the tests he or she takes.

Life gives us plenty of opportunities to fail, to make mistakes, to fall short, to lose.

What happens to turn the experience of having failed at something into a lingering "spirit of failure" in your soul? A spirit of failure usually develops from one of four main reasons:

1. Too Great a Burden of Responsibility

An experience of failure may be perceived by a person to be totally his or her fault. When that happens, a person often thinks of his failure as being unforgivable by other people or even by God, and he begins to think of himself as a failure. For example, a businessman may have lost his business—failing his employees, his customers, his vendors, and ultimately feeling as if he has failed his family and himself. Or a pastor may have lost his church—failing his congregation, his fellow pastors, himself, and feeling as if he has failed God.

Now, in all likelihood, no person is ever 100 percent at fault in the vast majority of cases. Other people, other forces, other influences, other factors are nearly always involved. If that is the case, the person who feels totally responsible is a person who is taking on too much responsibility and has assumed some false guilt.

Let me assure you of this—in the failure of a marriage, no one person is ever totally responsible for a divorce. Even if a person is abandoned or has a spouse commit adultery, the "innocent" person has at least a little bit of responsibility for failing to have determined at some point the character flaws in the person he or she married.

If there is any possibility that one or more people were involved in a failure or loss, a person needs to accept that fact and confess to God, "I confess to you my part of this failure. Please forgive me of my sin. Please teach me in my error. Please help me to overcome my mistake. Please give me the courage to move forward and not wallow in this failure for the rest of my life."

In other cases, and especially so in times of accidents or willful crimes, there may have been no other person involved. Sole responsibility for causing harm to another person may be a fact. In those cases, what a person needs to do is to own up to that failure and go to God, confessing, "I have sinned. I have erred. I was careless. Please forgive me for causing harm to another person. Please help me never to do anything like this again. Please give me the courage to face those who have been affected by my hurtful actions and to ask their forgiveness and make amends as best I can. Please wipe any tormenting memories from my mind, and help me to trust You to rebuild my life."

2. Too Much Pain

An experience of failure may be so painful that a person thinks to himself, I'm never going to try *that* again. The chance of losing is too painful to think about. When that happens, a spirit of failure develops.

I've met people who have found it so painful to have been abandoned by a spouse that they never want to even consider having a friendship with a person of the opposite sex. They have been burned, and they see themselves as having failed so completely in that area of their lives that they never want to risk being burned again.

Any time a person no longer wants to try to succeed, to make another attempt, to take another risk, or to open himself up to love again, a spirit of failure is present.

3. A Lingering Failure

A time of failure may have lingered so long in your life that you think it has become a permanent state. It's when you think a problem will never end that you develop a spirit of failure.

This often happens if the failure involves a human sickness, weakness, or addiction. Repeated failures at the same task or repeated failures to reach a desired goal can result in a spirit of failure.

I once heard a woman say, "I've tried to diet so many times I can't count them all. Each time I lose a little and then gain back even more. I'm just fat. I can't control my eating. I'm a terrible person." Her repeated attempts at trying to overcome what she perceived to be a flaw in her life left her feeling terrible about her entire life.

Be very careful that you don't extend a failure in one area of your life to other areas. This woman was wrong in her conclusion that just because she had failed at dieting, she was a terrible person. Yet that is very often what happens if a failure is repeated or if an experience of failure lingers over a long period of time.

By the way, this woman eventually learned why she overate and she learned a great deal about good nutrition; when that happened, she began to control her eating, and she lost weight!

In most cases, lingering failures and repeated failures can be remedied, healed, or the trend reversed—often through gaining information, receiving counseling, or engaging in a spiritual renewal process. Cry out to God about your lingering or repeated failures. Pray, "Lord, please help me! Show me what it is that I need to know, what I need to do, how I should respond. Lead me to the teacher, counselor, mentor, or advisor who can help me. Give me your wisdom on this. And help me not to think of myself as a failure in my whole life just because I have fallen short in one area of my life."

4. A Great or Severe Failure

A time of failure may be so great that a person concludes that his life is scarred forever and the failure has been "branded" permanently on his or her soul. This is often the case with those who have been convicted of crimes or who have had their failure widely publicized.

A person with a spirit of failure often gives himself or herself a label that depicts the failure associated with a past experience. For example, the person may say to himself or others,

"I'm a loser," "I'm a crook," "I'm an addict," "I'm a divorcee," or "I'm no good."

Any time a person feels trapped in the identity of a past failure, he has developed a spirit of failure.

If you believe your identity has been determined forever by a past experience of failure in your life, let me assure you that you are wrong. Jesus never desires that you bear any label of any kind other than the label He gives you: "Forgiven Saint and Beloved Child of God."

Your identity should be first and foremost "Christian." If you have not accepted Jesus as your Savior, do so today. Don't delay.

If you have accepted Jesus as your Savior, begin immediately to look yourself in the mirror and say, "Hello, Christian! Hello, Forgiven Saint."

Don't call yourself a criminal or even a former convict. Don't call yourself an addict or a recovered addict. Don't call yourself a prostitute or a former street walker. Call yourself what God calls you. See yourself as His beloved child, destined to live with Him forever in heaven. See yourself as being forgiven, filled with His Spirit, walking in faith.

The taking on of a new identity does not begin with what other people think or say about you. It doesn't begin with how other people react to you or act toward you. The taking on of a new identity begins with your believing in what Jesus has done for you and what God's Word says about you. It begins with how you think and speak about yourself. It begins with how you treat others and respond to others.

If you have taken on an identity associated with failure, cry out to God today, "Lord, I accept what Your Son did for me on the cross. I receive the Holy Spirit that Your Son Jesus promised to give me. I want to walk in the identity that Jesus has purchased for me with His shed blood. Help me now to see myself as You see me. Help me to walk in boldness according to what Your Word says about me. Renew my mind even as you renew my heart. Help me to treat others as the new creation that I am."

Job: A Case Study in Overcoming Failure

When we think of a person in the Bible who experienced great failure, it's difficult to think of someone who experienced more failure than Job.

The story of Job begins with a terrible loss in this man's life: all ten of his children—seven sons and three daughters—and many of his servants were killed. His many sheep, camels, oxen, and donkeys were all stolen by raiding bands of thieves.

Job lost his health. He developed painful boils from the top of his head to the soles of his feet.

Job then lost the respect of his wife who encouraged him to curse God and die.

He eventually did curse the day of his birth and fell into self-pity. He fell into negativity, unforgiveness, backbiting, and criticism as he argued with his so-called friends who came to give him counsel.

Did Job have a spirit of failure? Just read what he said about himself:

My spirit is broken, my days are extinguished, the grave is ready for me. (Job 17:1)

He [God] has made me a byword of the people, and I am one at whom men spit. (v. 6)

My days are past, my plans are torn apart, even the wishes of my heart. (v. 11)

Did Job have a murmuring spirit? Just read what he said about God:

His anger has torn me and hunted me down, He has gnashed at me with His teeth; my adversary glares at me.
(Job 16:9)

I was at ease, but He shattered me, and He has grasped me by the neck and shaken me to pieces; He has also set me up as His target. His arrows surround me. Without mercy He splits my kidneys open; He pours out my gall on the ground. He breaks through me with breach after breach; He runs at me like a warrior. (vv. 12–14)

He has cast me into the mire, and I have become like dust and ashes. (Job 30:19)

What turned things around for Job?

First, he recognized that his negative words and murmuring against God were futile. He saw his negative words and complaining for what they were—a form of rebellion against God. Job said, *"Even today my complaint is rebellion"* (Job 23:2).

Second, Job recognized that God had him precisely where He wanted him to be at that time and that in spite of his inability to see or understand the purposes of God, God was going to use this time to purify his life and make him stronger. Job said, *"He knows the way I take; when He has tried me, I shall come forth as gold"* (v. 10). He also said, *"What His soul desires, that He does. For He performs what is appointed for me"* (vv. 13–14).

Not only did Job recognize that God was in charge of his life, even in this period of great tribulation, but he submitted himself to hearing what God desired to say to him. He ceased his rebellious grumbling against God and said, *"Behold, I am insignificant; what can I reply to Thee? I lay my hand on my mouth....I will add no more"* (Job 40:4–5).

Third, Job determined deep within himself that no matter how hard things were in his life—no matter how much

Moving beyond a Spirit of Failure

loss he had experienced or how much his life seemed to be a failure on all fronts—he would not turn away from God, nor would he turn away from keeping the commandments of God. Job said,

> *Till I die I will not put away my integrity from me. I hold fast my righteousness and will not let it go. My heart does not reproach any of my days.* (Job. 27:5–6)

Fourth, Job repented of his past rebellion against God and voiced his faith in God. He said,

> *I know that Thou canst do all things, and that no purpose of Thine can be thwarted. Who is this that hides counsel without knowledge? Therefore I have declared that which I did not understand, things too wonderful for me, which I did not know...I have heard of Thee by the hearing of the ear; but now my eye sees Thee; therefore I retract, and I repent in dust and ashes.* (Job. 42:2–3, 5–6)

Fifth, Job did what the Lord asked him to do—pray for his friends. That act of praying for his friends was an act of forgiveness. The Lord made it clear that Job's friends had not spoken what was right about God and that their criticism of Job had been unfounded. The Lord made it clear that Job's friends had hurt Job and had caused him anguish. In praying for them, Job was forgiving them.

And what happened as a result of these actions on the part of Job? God's Word tells us that *"the Lord restored the fortunes of Job, and the Lord increased all that Job had twofold"* (v. 10).

Job received consolation from his brothers and his sisters and *"all who had known him before"*—and each person who came to comfort him gave him *"one piece of money, and each a ring of gold"* (v. 11). In the end, the Lord doubled his number of sheep, camels, oxen, and donkeys. He became the father of ten children—seven sons and three daughters. He lived one

241

hundred and forty years after his loss and died *"an old man and full of days"* (Job. 42:17).

The Bible makes it very clear that this particular time of trouble was a "test" of Job, but it was a test that the Lord had full confidence Job was going to pass. It was a test that would bring great reward. It was a test that Job would complete to the detriment of the devil.

Those are three very important truths you must keep in mind as you go through your difficult time.

God has a way through this time of failure. He expects you to go through this time, to pass this test, and to emerge stronger in faith, stronger in character, and stronger in your abilities.

God has a reward for you as you battle against and overcome a spirit of failure. Your greatest success still lies ahead of you! Your best days are still to come!

God knows that your overcoming a spirit of failure will give the devil a black eye. He knows that as you speak out of your faith and begin to take positive actions to walk in your faith, you are going to defeat the purposes the devil had for you. You are going to mess up the design he had for your life.

In the end, if you will persevere in your faith walk, God is going to bless you mightily. He will lead you, guide you, comfort you, encourage you, and reward you in ways that you can't even imagine right now.

Never lose sight of the potential for blessing that resides in the Lord. God's Word tells us, *"Now to Him who is able to do exceeding abundantly beyond all that we ask or think, according to the power* [of the Holy Spirit] *that works within us, to Him be the glory"* (Eph. 3:20–21).

If the devil can convince you that you are a failure—not just that you may have failed in a particular area of your life—he will have done a great deal to keep you from living in joy, peace, and blessing. He will have done a great deal to keep you from pursuing all that God has for you or receiving all that God desires to give you.

The Cure for a Spirit of Failure

Ultimately the cure for a spirit of failure is this: Use your faith! The problem you have with failure is ultimately a faith issue. The real question is, Are you going to continue to wallow in failure or are you going to walk in faith?

Use your faith to believe for three things:

1. Believe God Desires for You to Be Successful.

You must reject the lies of the devil about your failures and begin to believe that God has created you for success.

You may have failed in the past, but you are not a "failure."

You may have made mistakes, but you are not a mistake. I don't care about the origins of your birth or your ancestors or the sins of your parents. God caused you to be conceived and born on this earth for a high purpose—His purpose for your life is 100 percent good.

You may have sinned, but now that you have accepted Jesus Christ as your Savior, you are no longer a sinner, but rather a saint of the Most High God. I don't care how much you have sinned, how great your sin may have been, or how often you have sinned in the past. From the moment you accepted Jesus Christ as your Savior and began to follow Him as your Lord, you were put on a new path. The old path may have led to failure; the new path leads to success. The old path may have led to hell; the new path leads to heaven. The old path may have been marked by rebellion, error, and confusion; the new path is marked by obedience, right choices, and wise decisions.

God never told anyone in the Bible that he or she was a failure. He said about the Israelites—you are *chosen* by Me; you will be *blessed* by Me when you obey Me; you will be *multiplied*, and you and your families will be *preserved* by Me as you walk in My ways. God's plan was always for the increase and the success of His people.

If you do not believe that God desires good for you in your future, you will have little motivation to keep God's commandments or to walk in faith. You'll have a "What's the use?" attitude. And people with a "What's the use?" attitude are pretty much of no use to themselves, to others, or to the advancement of God's kingdom.

Believe that God wants to transform you, use you, bless you, and cause you to walk into a future that will be rewarding, fulfilling, and of great joy to you!

As much as God held out blessing as His desired destiny for His people, there was a second step the Israelites had to take to receive what God had promised to them.

2. Believe that Jesus **Is** the Answer.

Jesus truly is the answer to all life's problems, and because He *is* the answer, He has an answer or solution for your specific problem or need.

Jesus had an encounter with a woman who had lived with an *"issue of blood"* (Matt. 9:20 KJV) for twelve years. She was a woman who may very well have had all four of the above factors at work in her life.

This hemorrhage from her body not only left her weak physically but also caused her to be "unclean" in the eyes of society, which meant that she was shunned, even by close family members and friends. This woman knew great loss—in all likelihood, she hadn't even been *touched* by another human being for twelve years. She certainly must have felt emotional and physical pain or discomfort about her condition.

244

She also must have felt a heavy burden of responsibility associated with her illness. A person who was labeled as unclean in those days had the responsibility of "announcing" to others that they were unclean. That meant that every time this woman went out of her home or into the market she had to continually say, loudly enough for anybody within reasonable earshot to hear, "Unclean! Unclean!" Her words immediately caused others to move away from her. What terrible insult and rejection she must have felt in her soul. What a grave responsibility to think she might be the cause of others falling under the curse of being "unclean"!

This woman definitely had a long-standing experience in her loss of health. It's one thing to be sick for twelve hours. It's another thing to be sick for twelve days. It's horrible to be sick for twelve months. But to be sick to this extent for twelve years is almost unimaginable!

I have absolutely no doubt that after all that pain, bearing all that responsibility for continually announcing herself unclean, and having such a long-standing experience with loss led to this woman's opinion of herself as unclean, a failure in her society.

I have no doubt that she began to think of herself as untouchable, incurable, undesirable, unwanted. Those are very often the emotions of those who have a spirit of failure.

But, thank God, one day she heard about Jesus! And in spite of all that she had felt in the past, she made her way to Him. She inched her way through the crowd, very likely even getting down on her hands and knees to worm her way through the masses that surrounded Jesus. And she reached out and touched the hem of His garment in faith.

Her faith rose up in her and her faith drove her to Jesus.

This woman with the hemorrhage for twelve years got her thinking squared away. She said, *"If I just touch His garments, I shall get well"* (Mark 5:28). Note that word *"shall."* She was believing without doubt. Her goal was clearly in mind. She believed, *"I shall get well."*

Are you believing today that you *shall* receive what God says He has promised to you in His Word?

You may be eating ketchup sandwiches, but the thought in your mind and the words out of your mouth must become, "I *am* having all my needs met by Christ Jesus. I *shall* prosper."

You may be lying on a hospital bed receiving chemotherapy, but the thought in your mind and the words out of your mouth must become, "I *am* being healed. I *shall* be made whole in Christ Jesus."

You may be sitting in a room, waiting for a judge to give pronouncement on your case, but the thought in your mind and the words out of your mouth must be, "I *am* loved by God, and I *shall* be healed from *any* ill effects of this experience in my life."

You might be broke, busted, or disgusted, but you must keep saying, "My faith is in the Lord. He's going to bring me out of this situation."

Genuine faith always drives us toward Jesus, not away from Him. Faith will compel you to get up and get yourself to church. Faith will urge you to open your Bible and begin to read it again. Faith will cause you to drop to your knees and cry out to God.

And the good news is this—Jesus always responds to our faith.

How do I know that faith was at work in this woman's story? Because Jesus said, *"Someone did touch Me, for I was aware that power had gone out of Me"* (Luke 8:46). When the woman saw that she had been discovered, Jesus called her to Himself and He said to her, *"Daughter, your faith has made you well; go in peace"* (v. 48).

There's no feeling of "burden" or responsibility for a failure that Jesus can't help you shoulder or lift from your shoulders.

There's no pain associated with failure that is too deep for Jesus to heal.

There's no lingering or repeated failure that Jesus cannot give you the wisdom and courage to overcome.

There's no failure that is too great that Jesus cannot change your identity from that of "failure" to that of "success."

3. Believe that Obedience Brings Reward.

"Doing things God's way" brings blessing.

Obedience is absolutely required if a believer is going to move toward success. You must make up your mind, and settle the issue in your heart, that you are going to choose to do things God's way rather than your own way, the world's way, or the devil's way.

Here is what the Lord said to His people then, and what He says to His people now,

> If you will diligently obey the LORD your God, being careful to do all His commandments which I command you today, the LORD your God will set you high above all the nations of the earth. And all these blessings shall come upon you and overtake you, if you will obey the LORD your God.
> (Deut. 28:1–2)

> The LORD will make you abound in prosperity, in the offspring of your body and in the offspring of your beast and in the produce of your ground, in the land which the LORD swore to your fathers to give you. The LORD will open for you His good storehouse, the heavens, to give rain to your land in its season and to bless all the work of your hand;

247

and you shall lend to many nations, but you shall not borrow. And the LORD shall make you the head and not the tail, and you only shall be above, and you shall not be underneath, if you will listen to the commandments of the LORD your God, which I charge you today, to observe them carefully. (Deut. 28:11–13)

Nobody stumbles into obedience. Nobody lucks into living a righteous life. Obedience is a choice you must make, and can make. The pursuit of doing things God's way is a choice that is set before you.

Again, here is what the Lord said to His people and continues to say to you and me today,

I have set before you today life and prosperity, and death and adversity; in that I command you today to love the LORD your God, to walk in His ways and to keep His commandments and His statutes and His judgments, that you may live and multiply, and that the LORD your God may bless you in the land where you are entering to possess it....I call heaven and earth to witness against you today, that I have set before you life and death, the blessing and the curse. So choose life in order that you may live, you and our descendants, by loving the LORD your God, by obeying His voice, and by holding fast to Him; for this is your life and the length of your days, that you may live in the land which the LORD swore to your fathers. (Deut. 30:15–16,19–20)

God's Word also gives us the flip side of obedience. If we refuse to put God first, we are subject to His chastisement, which at times can be very harsh. In fact, the greater our resistance to obeying God, the greater the chastisement always seems to be!

The Lord said to His people then, and He says to us today, *"If you will not obey the LORD your God, to observe to do all His commandments and His statutes with which I charge you today, that all these curses shall come upon you and overtake you"* (Deut. 28:15). And then, the Lord gave a long list of severe troubles that would come upon the people. He warned,

> *The LORD will send upon you curses, confusion, and rebuke, in all you undertake to do, until you are destroyed and until you perish quickly, on account of the evil of your deeds, because you have forsaken Me.* (v. 20)

If you truly want to overcome a spirit of failure, you are going to have to resolve deep within your spirit, "I am going to obey God. I'm going to stop doing things my way and start doing things God's way. I am going to put God first in my life."

Do you truly want to live free of failure? Start believing, speaking, and building your life based upon the truths that God has a success plan for you, Jesus *is* the answer to all your needs, and a life of obedience brings reward. If you believe, speak, and live out these truths, you will move beyond your failures into His perfect plan for you.

15

Moving beyond
Past Sins and Habits

One of the saddest statements in the entire Bible was made by Jesus as part of His description of the last days. He said,

Just as it happened in the days of Noah, so it shall be also in the days of the Son of Man: they were eating, they were drinking, they were marrying, they were being given in marriage, until the day that Noah entered the ark, and the flood came and destroyed them all. It was the same as happened in the days of Lot: they were eating, they were drinking, they were buying, they were selling, they were planting, they were building; but on the day that Lot went out from Sodom it rained fire and brimstone from heaven and destroyed them all. It will be just the same on the day that the Son of Man is revealed. On that day, let not the one who is on the housetop and whose goods are in the house go down to take them away; and likewise let not the one who is in the field turn back. Remember Lot's wife. Whoever seeks to keep his life shall lose it, and whoever loses his life shall preserve it. (Luke 17:26–33)

Remember Lot's wife.

"Remember Lot's wife."

What sadness is bound up in those words!

Things to Remember...and Things to Forget

There are some things we are to remember, and there are some things we are to let go of and forget.

We are to remember who we are in Christ Jesus—that's something we are to remember every hour for the rest of our lives. We are to remember what Jesus did for us on the cross. We are to remember how God has protected us and provided for us in the past. We are to remember that sin has deadly consequences and that we have been given the power to withstand any temptation that comes our way. We are to remember God's promises and His commandments. We are to remember that Jesus said He is coming again.

There are many things that God calls us to remember. We are to regulate and plan and live out our lives on the basis of these things that we remember. We are not to become discouraged in any of these things that are good and right for us to remember.

What should we remember? Psalm 103 tells us to *"forget none of His benefits"* (v. 2), and then the psalmist gives us a list:

• Don't forget that He has pardoned your sins.

• Don't forget that He has healed you.

• Don't forget that He redeems your life from the pit.

• Don't forget that He has crowned you with His loving kindness and compassion.

• Don't forget that He is the One who satisfied your years with good things.

• Don't forget that He renews you.

• Don't forget that He performs righteous deeds.

• Don't forget that He judges those who oppress you.

If you set your mind and heart to remembering all that the Lord has done for you, is doing in you, and will do all around you, you won't have time to feel depressed, angry, bitter, or vengeful!

But there are other things we are to forget—we are to walk away and forget those things that will tie us down to past sinful habits, slow us down in our spiritual growth, or push us down into failure, fear, or worry.

We must forget—and quit talking about—our past sin once we have confessed it to God and been forgiven of it.

When we bring to our minds and to our lips the sins of our past, we are demonstrating that we have not forgiven ourselves for what happened. Oh, we may believe we have God's forgiveness. But we haven't forgiven ourselves. We are continually reminding ourselves of our sins because we haven't truly been able to release them.

It's a terrible thing to keep remembering what God has forgotten. The Lord tells us that when we confess our sins, He forgives us and then He forgets our sin. Our sin is completely blotted out of any heavenly record. God remembers our sin only when we bring it up to Him again! (See 1 John 1:9 and Psalm 103:12.)

One of the most wonderful passages you can plant into your spirit are these words from Psalm 103:

He has not dealt with us according to our sins, nor rewarded us according to our iniquities. For as high as the heavens are above the earth, so great is His lovingkindness toward those who fear Him. As far as the east is from the west, so far has He removed our transgressions from us. Just as a father has compassion on his children, so the Lord has compassion on those who fear Him. (vv. 10–13)

So many times I have heard people say,

253

"If I just hadn't gone to jail..."

"If I just hadn't been divorced..."

"If I just hadn't started smoking pot..."

"If I just hadn't gone to that party..."

Any time you start living in an "if I just" frame of mind, you are looking back!

Lot's wife *"looked back."* That was her downfall.

God had provided a way of escape for Lot and his entire family when the time came for His judgment to fall on Sodom and Gomorrah. When Lot hesitated to leave the city, the Lord sent angels to forcibly lead Lot, his wife, and his daughters by the hand and accompany them to the edge of town and then command them, *"Escape for your life! Do not look behind you, and do not stay anywhere in the valley; escape to the mountains, lest you be swept away"* (Gen. 19:17).

When the brimstone and fire from the Lord began to fall on those wicked cities of Sodom and Gomorrah, Lot's wife *"from behind him, looked back; and she became a pillar of salt"* (v. 26).

She became covered up and encrusted by the brimstone that was falling from heaven. She became completely immobilized in her position of yearning for her past life. There are some Bible scholars who believe that this phrase *"looked back"* actually means that she had turned and was starting to walk back toward her home in Sodom when the judgment fell. She had made a decision to go back to the life she had known, rather than obey the Lord and pursue the future that He had authorized for her to have.

Jesus said, *"Remember Lot's wife."*

We don't know what Mrs. Lot longed for. It may have been a possession she left behind, perhaps a secret lover, perhaps her position in the society there. Something there still had a hold on her heart.

She was out of Sodom, but Sodom wasn't out of her.

How true that is for many people today!

When the Lord brings you out of something in your past—don't look back! The enemy will always try to pull you back into the slime and miry clay of your past. The truth of God is that He has delivered you from Sodom. It's up to you to walk toward your future and not slide back to your past. You are out of your past—it's behind you. Make sure your past is out of you!

Mrs. Lot was right on the brink of experiencing the best days of her life. She was on the verge of being totally delivered from one of the most wicked cities on the earth. From Abraham's conversation with the Lord, we know that there weren't ten righteous people in the entire city! (See Genesis 18:32–33.) The city was debased and wicked through and through with all kinds of sin and perversion, and she was about to be set free from all that. She was on the verge of being delivered from one of the most powerful acts of judgment found in the entire Bible. She was on the edge of moving into the good things that God had for her and her family.

But she looked back, and in looking back, she was destroyed. Any time God sets you free from any bondage, any perversion, any addiction, there's great danger in your looking back to that sin.

Your past has no hold on you—unless you allow it to have a hold.

Your past cannot dominate you—unless you allow it to dominate you.

Your past cannot influence your choices and your decisions—unless you allow that to be the case.

If you allow your past to rise up in your mind and capture your imagination, fantasies, daydreams, and desires, you will turn back to your past—and, in doing so, your past may very well destroy you.

Your Best Days Are Still Ahead

You may have some fond memories of people you knew in your sinful past, but if you allow those memories to take you back into active relationships with those people, you will endanger your future.

You may find yourself remembering the "good times," but if you allow those memories to pull you back into those circumstances, you will put your God-promised destiny in jeopardy.

Give up those old memories. Start making new ones that are God-pleasing, God-authorized, and God-promised! If you are going to move forward, there are some things and some relationships you need to leave behind.

Mrs. Lot's turning back may seem like a little thing, but it's the little things that can ensnare us and trip us up—that little hug, that little glance, that little conversation, that little drink, that little bit of drugs, that little flirtation, that little lie, that little deceit, that little item you shoplifted, that little cover-up, that little encounter. Remember Lot's wife!

It's Time to Say Good-Bye

It's time a lot of folks wave good-bye to their past, so they can say hello to the future God has in store for them!

Once we are saved, it is our responsibility to say good-bye to...

- Every shady deal
- Every form of corruption
- Every form of witchcraft
- Every drug dealer
- Every bad relationship

It is our responsibility to declare, "I will trust in the Lord with all my heart, and I will not lean on my own wisdom or understanding." (See Proverbs 3:5.)

You may have been a drug user in the past, but once you are in Christ Jesus, drugs are not to rule your life. Christ Jesus rules your life. The old thing that had you enslaved is in the past. The "newness" of your life in Christ is yours, both now and to come.

You may have been promiscuous in the past, but once you are in Christ Jesus, sexual passion should not rule your life. Christ Jesus is in control. The old way of behaving is in your past. A new godly way of relating sexually is part of your present and your future.

You may have been involved in stealing from others, but once you are in Christ Jesus, your lust for "things" and your disregard for the laws of man and God are no longer the driving forces in your life. Christ Jesus is in the driver's seat. The old way of behaving is over. A new way of dealing with possessions—both your own and those of other people—is in operation now.

You may have been involved in the occult in the past, but once you are in Christ Jesus, the psychics, the tarot cards, and the daily horoscope are not the dictators of your future. Christ Jesus is the One who leads and guides you according to the power of His Holy Spirit at work in you. The old way of approaching life is over. A new way of planning your day and ordering your priorities has taken its place.

You may have been involved in a false religion in the past, or you may have attended some sort of "religious meeting" in which you heard very bad teaching about God, but once you are in Christ Jesus, the false religions are no longer the foundation for your belief system. You are in relationship with Christ Jesus, and you function according to what is pleasing to Him as your Savior and Lord. The old way of ritualistic, rule-bound religion is over. A new way of grace and freedom and willing service to the Lord is your future.

In like manner, you may have been shackled in your innermost soul by deep feelings of rejection, anger, hatred, bitterness, or any number of other negative feelings because of what happened to you in the past. Once you are in Christ Jesus, these negative emotions are not to be the driving force of your life. The emotions and character traits of a Spirit-led, Spirit-filled life are part of your present and your future!

The apostle Paul described this new life in his letter to the Colossians. He said first of all that this new life is available to all who believe, without any regard to their race, culture, past religion, or social status. He said, *"There is no distinction between Greek and Jew, circumcised and uncircumcised, barbarian, Scythian, slave and freeman, but Christ is all, and in all"* (Col. 3:11). In writing to the Galatians, Paul said, *"There is neither Jew nor Greek, there is neither slave nor free man, there is neither male nor female; for you are all one in Christ Jesus"* (Gal. 3:28).

Paul then went on to give a description of the *new* emotions and behaviors that are to be manifested by us as believers in Christ Jesus:

> *Those who have been chosen of God, holy and beloved, put on a heart of compassion, kindness, humility, gentleness and patience; bearing with one another, and forgiving each other, whoever has a complaint against anyone; just as the Lord forgave you, so also should you. And beyond all these things put on love, which is the perfect bond of unity. And let the peace of Christ rule in your hearts, to which indeed you were called in one body; and be thankful. Let the word of Christ richly dwell within you, with all wisdom teaching and admonishing one another with psalms and hymns and spiritual songs, singing with thankfulness in your hearts to God. And whatever you do in word or deed, do all in the name of the Lord Jesus, giving thanks through Him to God the Father.* (Col. 3:12–17)

Your Past Does Not Dictate Your Future

Let me make this very clear: Your past does not dictate your future once you are in Christ Jesus.

Your past may have dictated your future before you came to Christ. In fact, before you came to Christ, your past experiences became the very basis for your attitudes, opinions, perspectives on life, belief system, and even your automatic responses to various types of situations and circumstances.

Now, as a new creature in Christ Jesus, your past does not dictate your future. But what you *believe* about the Word of God does dictate your future!

If you continue to think as the old creature thought, you will speak as the old creature and act as the old creature did.

If you continue to dwell on the past, if you continue to "relive" the sins of your past, if you continue to buy into the errors and lies of your past, you will not be renewed.

You Must Choose to Be Renewed

Renewal of your mind and heart is not an automatic process. However, the *opportunity* to be renewed is an automatic result of your being saved and filled with God's Spirit. Your state of being as a new creature is automatic. But the renewal of your mind is something you are challenged to do.

God's Word says,

> *Do not lie to one another, since you laid aside the old self with its evil practices, and have put on the new self who is being renewed to a true knowledge according to the image of the One who created him.*　　　(Col. 3:9–10)

We are the ones who do the putting off and the putting on. This isn't the only place in the Bible where we read this. Let these passages of God's Word sink deep into your mind and heart:

> *Do not be conformed to this world, but be transformed by the renewing of your mind, that you may prove what the will of God is, that which is good and acceptable and perfect.*
> 　　　(Rom. 12:2)

Put on the Lord Jesus Christ, and make no provision for the flesh in regard to its lusts.   (Rom. 13:14)

All of you who were baptized into Christ have clothed yourselves with Christ.   (Gal. 3:27)

Those who belong to Christ Jesus have crucified the flesh with its passions and desires. If we live by the Spirit, let us also walk by the Spirit.   (Gal. 5:24–25)

This I say therefore, and affirm together with the Lord, that you walk no longer just as the Gentiles also walk, in the futility of their mind, being darkened in their understanding, excluded from the life of God, because of the ignorance that is in them, because of the hardness of their heart; and they, having become callous, having given themselves over to sensuality, for the practice of every kind of impurity with greediness. But you did not learn Christ in this way, if indeed you have heard Him and have been taught in Him, just as truth is in Jesus, that, in reference to your former manner of life, you lay aside the old self, which is being corrupted in accordance with the lusts of deceit, and that you be renewed in the spirit of your mind, and put on the new self, which in the likeness of God has been created in righteousness and holiness of the truth.   (Eph. 4:17–24)

Again and again, God's Word challenges us: *"clothe yourself in Christ," "put on the new self," "walk by the Spirit,"* and *"be renewed in the spirit of your mind."* It is our responsibility to *"crucify the old self," "put off the old man,"* and to choose not to *"be conformed to this world."*

We are the ones who do the putting off and putting on. We are the ones who must say "no" to the devil, the world, and the impulses of the flesh, and say "yes" to the Holy Spirit's guidance. We are the ones who must say "no" to the lies we have been taught and the lies that continue to come against us, and say "yes" to the Word of God.

Nobody else will do this for you. In truth, nobody else can do it for you. Your pastor can't do it for you. Your spouse can't do it for you. Your parent or grandparent or Bible teacher or Sunday school teacher can't do it for you.

You and you alone are responsible for choosing what you will do with the Word of God and for choosing how you will obey the Holy Spirit's commands to your spirit.

We each are responsible for choosing whether we will believe God's Word and whether we will apply the Word of God to our own lives and live out its truth in our daily choices, decisions, conversations, and deeds.

Nobody is going to read the Bible for you.

Nobody is going to memorize Bible verses for you.

Nobody is going to attend a Bible study for you or listen to Bible teaching tapes for you.

And nobody is going to *believe* the Word of God for you.

Nobody is going to look for ways in which you can put what the Bible teaches into practical, concrete use in your life except *you*.

Nobody is going to speak the Word of God out of your lips except *you*.

It is 100 percent up to you to believe the Word of God, study it, speak it, and live it out!

The good news is that as you do believe, read and study, speak, and live out the Word of God, you are changed.

Stop wishing for the past.

Stop talking about your past.

Stop dwelling on the past.

Start believing and hoping and planning and talking about your future! If you quit looking back, God will show you what He has for you today and for your future.

There's No Pleasure for You There

You cannot go back to your sinful past and find pleasure. It simply isn't there!

I guarantee you this—if you go back to a particular sin that had you in bondage in the past, you will not enjoy that sin. The believer in Christ Jesus will not, cannot, and does not enjoy that former sin the way he once did. Why? Because the born-again believer has the Holy Spirit resident inside him, and the Holy Spirit will not allow him to feel comfortable in a sinful situation or feel satisfied in any way by sinning.

You may be drawn to that ol' crack house, but as a believer, you have been empowered by the Holy Spirit to drive the other way.

You may think about visiting that old girlfriend, but as a believer, you have been empowered by the Holy Spirit with the ability to put down the phone before you dial her number.

You may fantasize about picking up that liquor bottle, but you are empowered by the Holy Spirit to pour that liquor down the drain and never enter another liquor store again.

The unbeliever has a desire to sin that can be so over-whelmingly powerful that he or she can hardly say "no" to a temptation. The genuine believer has no desire to sin, and when temptation comes, he or she has the privilege to call upon the Holy Spirit to receive power to resist that temptation.

The Bible tells us that the Israelites missed Egypt—among the things they missed were the spicy things: leeks, onions, and garlic. (See Numbers 11:5.) Many people who come to Christ start to miss the things they remember as giving spice to their lives—the sin that made things a little more exciting and pleasurable and intriguing. They long for the things they remember as being tantalizing, sensual, and enticing.

Some folks have a bad memory.

There's nothing truly satisfying about sin. There's nothing nourishing or fun about sin in the long run of life—and especially the long run of eternity! The devil's lie is that what you used to do on Saturday night is far more interesting and fun than what you are doing on Sunday morning. The devil never tells you the full consequences of sin. He never points out the hangover, the crash, the broken heart, the smashed family relationships, the destroyed career, the wasted finances, the sickness, or the stench of death that come from sin. He'll remind you of the initial, momentary, and very brief pleasure of sin. That's the bait. The hook inside that bait, however, is deadly.

The devil's lie will be, "Girl, you're too young to be sitting home on Saturday night. You should be partying."

The devil's lie will be, "You're too much of a man for this church stuff."

The devil's lie will be, "Remember how good this used to make you feel?"

He'll never remind you that your old boyfriend used to hit you and steal money from your purse; that your old girlfriend cheated on you at every opportunity, even with your best friend; that your drug habit took every bit of the money you thought would one day go for a car and a house.

The devil will tell you that you are never going to be happy again, that things will never change, and that you will never experience anything better than what you've known in the past. The devil is a liar! The Lord has said,

I will make up to you for the years that the swarming locust has eaten, the creeping locust, the stripping locust, and the gnawing locust, My great army which I sent among you. And you shall have plenty to eat and be satisfied, and praise the name of the LORD your God, who has dealt wondrously with you; then My people will never be put to shame.

(Joel 2:25–26)

When a drug addict says, "I can't stop doing drugs," he's believing the lie of the devil.

When a man says, "I can't stop having sex with every willing girl I take out," he's believing the lie of the devil.

When a woman says, "I can't stop myself from purchasing something in the store that I really want," she's believing the lie of the devil.

The truth of God is that He has already destroyed that addiction, that sin, that bondage!

Know the truth! Accept the truth! Believe the truth!

And then, begin to act on the truth.

Declare out loud to yourself, "It's over!" That bondage to sin is over. You now have the ability to make a decision to yield your life to the Holy Spirit and say "no" to any temptation that comes your way.

I can recount numerous instances to you in which I know with certainty in my spirit that God closed certain doors so people would not go back to the bondage they once experienced.

It's no mystery to me that Frank's former drug dealer was murdered.

It's no coincidence to me that Shawna's former husband remarried.

It's no wonder to me that Lavelle's former lover moved out of town and didn't leave a forwarding address or phone number.

There are some situations, and some relationships, that God simply doesn't want His people to go back to once they are saved. God not only wants to forgive His people, He wants to deliver them from evil.

Know the truth! Accept the truth! Believe the truth!

And then, begin to act on the truth.

Declare out loud to yourself, "It's over!" That bondage to sin is over. You now have the ability to make a decision to yield your life to the Holy Spirit and say "no" to any temptation that comes your way.

It's Time to Go Forth!

God spoke to Abraham,

Go forth from your country, and from your relatives, and from your father's house, to the land which I will show you; and I will make you a great nation, and I will bless you, and make your name great, and so you shall be a blessing; and I will bless those who bless you, and the one who curses you I will curse. And in you all the families of the earth shall be blessed. (Gen. 12:1–3)

Abraham was about seventy-five years old when God spoke this to him—proof enough that it's never too old for God to call a person out of bondage into a new life.

God said He would show Abraham a new land. He promised to make him a great nation and to give him a great name in history. The Lord promised to bless him, to bless those who blessed him, and to make him a blessing to the whole earth.

God has this same future for you! His desire is that you leave behind anything in your past that has been holding you back into sinful bondage and move forward to the place He will show you. He promises to use you and give importance and value to your life. He promises to bless you in every way and to bless those around you who help you. He promises to drive the enemy of your soul far from you. He promises to make you a blessing to others. That's your destiny in Christ Jesus. That's what God has for you.

But you've got to do the "going forth" from your past.

Abraham would have received nothing of God's promises if he hadn't obeyed God. We wouldn't be reading about

Abraham today if he hadn't done what God said to do. The good news is that Abraham *"went forth as the LORD had spoken to him"* (Gen. 12:4).

Abraham did what he was commanded to do—and God did what He had promised to do!

That's the principle God calls us to follow today. We do what He commands us to do, and God does what He promises to do!

Read what God's Word says on this:

Do not call to mind the former things, or ponder things of the past. Behold, I will do something new, now it will spring forth; will you not be aware of it? I will even make a roadway in the wilderness, rivers in the desert.
(Isa. 43:18–19)

He who is blessed in the earth shall be blessed by the God of truth; and he who swears in the earth shall swear by the God of truth; because the former troubles are forgotten, and because they are hidden from My sight! (Isa. 65:16)

Behold, I create new heavens and a new earth; and the former things shall not be remembered or come to mind. But be glad and rejoice forever in what I create.
(vv. 17–18)

What is it that you need to leave behind today?

What is it that you need to be loosed from?

What is it that you need to break free from?

Years ago I went through a situation in my life when I lost everything I had. I said to the Lord, "This isn't fair. I've been 'sold out' to You. I'm 100 percent committed to you."

The Lord spoke back into my heart, "Son, give up your past. And I will give you a new future."

Moving beyond Past Sins and Habits

Even if you have been hurt, even if you have been treated unfairly, even if you have been dealt a terrible blow, even if you have suffered great loss, quit looking back to those difficult days. Start looking ahead to the future God has for you!

Once you move beyond yesterday's pain, you'll discover that your best days are still ahead!

Conclusion

Keep Your Eyes on the Goal

The apostle Paul wrote, *"I have fought the good fight, I have finished the course, I have kept the faith; in the future there is laid up for me the crown of righteousness"* (2 Tim. 4:7–8).

Paul wrote those words toward the end of his life. His personal testimony pointed to the enduring power of his faith. Paul never gave up. It wasn't at the end of his life that he realized that a crown of righteousness lay ahead for him. Paul knew that from the moment he received Christ Jesus as his Savior!

What gave Paul his willingness to keep on fighting the good fight? His faith that the Lord had a crown of righteousness ahead for him.

What compelled Paul to finish the course laid out for him by the Lord? His faith that the Lord had a crown of righteousness ahead for him.

What caused Paul never to quit believing in the Lord Jesus and never to quit sharing the Gospel with others? His faith that the Lord had a crown of righteousness ahead for him.

"But what," you may ask, "is so important about a crown of righteousness?"

A crown of righteousness means *victory.*

A crown of righteousness means that you are in right standing with God—and those who are in right standing with God are those who are in position to receive *all* the eternal rewards and *all* the earthly blessings that God has for them!

Paul knew that he would be victorious in overcoming every obstacle and that he was going to receive *absolutely everything* that God had promised to Him and had laid up for Him in His storehouse—both now and in the eternal future.

Your faith has been given to you by God to take you somewhere. It has been given to you so you can move right on past all the enemy's obstacles that try to slow you down, push you down, pull you down, or bring you down. It has been given to you so you can press forward in your life toward the *fullness* of *every blessing* that God has for you. It has been given to you so you can endure as you keep on walking...and keep on walking...and keep on walking all the way to the finish line in heaven.

Don't give up now. You're one step closer to the rewards and blessings that God has for you! Remember, your *best* days are still ahead!

About the Author

Dennis Leonard is an accomplished author, the CEO and founder of Legacy Publishers International, has produced 2 gospel albums under his label Praizia Music and is the senior pastor/founder of Heritage Christian Center in Denver, CO, one of the most ethnically diverse congregations in America with over 12,000 in weekly attendance. His daily and weekly television broadcasts are aired in several markets nationally. He is also Bishop of Multi-Cultural Ministries for the Full Gospel Baptist Church Fellowship.

Other Titles by DENNIS LEONARD

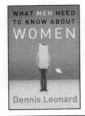

Dennis Leonard has filled the pages of this comprehensive book with solid biblical principles that cut straight to the core of that often illusive relationship between men and women. These are principles you will want to read again and again as you take the hand of the woman you love and walk together in your calling as joint heirs of the grace of life. 1-880809-51-6

In his newest book, *Happiness Matters*, Dennis Leonard explores the principles that produce happiness, the negative habits that strip happiness from our lives, and the relationship between happiness and that wondrous gift of God's Holy Spirit-joy.

1-880809-63-X

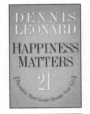

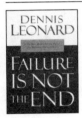

This book is solid and carefully targeted Bible-based discipleship framed in a 30-day "life makeover" plan to help you overcome your past and step into your God-ordained destiny. It will help you make strategic and biblical course corrections that will set you on track for the journey of pursuing your life's purpose. 1-880809-43-5

Financial insecurity is the #1 cause of stress, loss and breakdown in families and relationships today. Learn how to assess your financial condition, learn new money management habits, how to build a financial plan and how to grow in wealth and prosperity.

1-880809-20-6

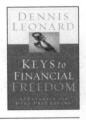

Your Best Days Are Still Ahead reveals powerful principles that release you to walk in the freedom that belongs to you as a child of God. It's time to move beyond your self-imposed boundaries. Learn how you can break free from the past and master the keys to your future.
1-880809-53-2 • *Spanish* 1-880809-55-9

You cannot change where you have been, but you can change where you are going. *Don't Judge My Future By My Past* offers encouragement and hope for everyone held back by their past. No matter what our past, with God's help we can put it behind us and move into a future brighter than anything we have ever imagined.

1-880809-15-X